ARTS OF RUSSIA

Kira Kornilovich
Abraam Kaganovich

ARTS OF RUSSIA

From the Origins to the End of the 18th Century

Translated from the Russian by James Hogarth
124 illustrations in colour; 58 illustrations in black and white

NAGEL PUBLISHERS GENEVA-PARIS-MUNICH

Publisher's Note

The preparation of our various publications on Russia had drawn our attention to the lack of any general study of the history of Russian art; and the present work is designed to fill that gap.

We need not stress the difficulty of collecting illustrative material on the artistic work produced throughout the vast extent of Russian territory; and we are correspondingly grateful to all those who have assisted us in our arduous quest and have played a part, in either a private or an official capacity, in making possible the production of this work.

In the first place we should like to thank Mr V.A. Ankudinov, President of the Directorate of Foreign Tourism attached to the Council of Ministers of the U.S.S.R., who used the high authority of his office to give us every possible assistance.

Our gratitude is also due to Mr B. Piotrovsky, Director of the Hermitage Museum, to Mrs V. Berezina and Mr V.G. Lukonin, Keepers in that Museum, for much helpful advice.

We should also like to thank M. B. Lossky, Conservateur of the Musée National du Château de Fontainebleau, for his valuable assistance.

I The Beginnings

In the first millennium A.D., in that distant time before there was any thought of an entity called the Russian people, the territory which was later to be the land of Rus or Russia was occupied by numerous tribes of Eastern Slavs who lived by hunting, fishing and to some extent by farming. Archaeological investigation has shown that they also possessed the rudiments of the art of building, for excavation has brought to light the remains of ancient settlements surrounded by earthen ramparts and stout timber palisades. (It is significant that the Russian word for town, *gorod*, originally meant an enclosed settlement).

In the construction of their simple dwellings these Slavonic tribes used a variety of materials. In the Dnieper area, for example, the houses were usually built in pisé; in the forest regions of the north-east they were of timber. (Here again we find echoes of the past in the Russian language: for example *zodchy*, an architect, comes from the Slavonic word for clay, and *plotnik*, a carpenter, comes from the word for a raft of logs).

The Slavs were pagans; and, as with other pagans, their gods were incarnations of the forces of nature and the elements who controlled the destinies of men and presided over all forms of human activity. The chief deities in the Slavonic pantheon were Dazhdbog the sun god (also known as Svarog or Khors or Yarila, for different tribes gave him different names); the god of the Winds, Stribog; Perun the Thunderer; the Earth Goddess; and Mokosh, the goddess of water. The Slavs also worshipped Radunitsa the goddess of spring and the patron divinities of love, the eternally youthful Lada and Lel. Indeed the list of their divinities is endless, for every corner of the visible world was peopled with a host of minor gods and spirits. The house was the domain of the diminutive house-demon; wells were inhabited by the well-sprite, rivers and lakes by the *rusalka* or water-nymph; in the forests lived the wood-demon; and the tracks used by animals and even the roads trodden by humans were haunted at night by Kashchey the Deathless and the nightmare hag Baba-Yaga who flew through the air in a mortar propelled by a pestle.

We know that the Slavs made sculptured representations of their divinities. The wooden statues which are mentioned by the chroniclers have not survived, but archaeologists have found a number of small figurines, both male and female, made of bronze, pottery or stone. Some of the stone images were of considerable size. All these works, however, are extremely primitive.

These statues were set up in sacred groves, and probably also in temples. The chronicler, at any rate, refers to "idols' houses" or shrines. We have some evidence about the Slavs of the Baltic area which indicates that these shrines were built of timber. Of building in stone we have so far only a single example—the remains of an oval structure built in grey sandstone which were found during excavations in the oldest part of Kiev in 1908. Most scholars agree in regarding this as a pagan temple.

The material which has come down to us in greatest quantity from this period consists of artefacts such as domestic utensils, weapons, and ornaments in great variety *(Plates pp. 9 above, 9 below, 10, 11)*. Perhaps only the articles in this last group, however, can be regarded as works of art. They include buckles and pendants—often made in the form of grotesque schematic figurines of animals and humans—as well as necklaces, bracelets and rings: all the trifles, in fact, which from time immemorial down to our own day have beguiled the vanity of men and women. Occasionally we find objects cast in silver, which are sometimes gilded, but usually they are made of bronze, stone or glass; the glass is sometimes gilded or coloured with metal oxides.

The great bulk of these articles were found during the excavation of funerary *kurgans* (earthen mounds erected over the remains of the dead). There is nothing surprising about this. The ancient Slavs shared the general pagan belief in a life beyond the grave which was similar in all respects to life on earth. Accordingly they took with them into the grave all that they had loved during their earthly existence and would need in their future life—their wife, their favourite horse, their weapons, their household goods. The dead man was clad in his finest raiment, his "wedding garments". Nothing less than this was conceivable, for when he appeared before the immortal gods he must present himself in all the magnificence he had enjoyed in life.

The artistic culture of the Eastern Slavs was the infancy of Russian art, but it prepared the ground for the later flowering of that art. The rapid development in ancient Russia of timber building, decorative woodcarving and metalworking was the result of many centuries' experience in the carpenter's craft, in carving and in metalworking, including the handling of precious metals. Many of the patterns created by these early craftsmen, in which a complex design of vegetable motifs and scrollwork is curiously combined with schematic representations of human beings and animals—varied in the course of time and enriched by new themes—have remained as basic elements in the repertoire of Russian ornament. They were common in folk art at the beginning of the 20th century, and are still found even in our own day in painting, woodcarving and above all in embroidery.

II Kiev, Mother of Russian Cities

The irresistible advance of history sweeps away everything in its path. In due course the tribal system, with its patriarchal way of life, passed into limbo; and at the end of the 9th century and in the 10th the first Russian feudal state, the Princedom of Kiev, grew up on the ruins of the older world.

A new social order now came into being and made its influence felt in many directions. The land increasingly fell into the hands of large proprietors, and the gulf between rich and poor, between the nobility and the ordinary people, became ever wider. The artistic life of the princedom now developed in the towns, which steadily increased in number: at the end of the 9th century there were twenty-five, by the end of the 11th century two hundred. The development of a class structure in society determined the character of building in these towns: side by side with the hovels of the craftsmen and the poorer classes stood the substantial dwellings of the more prosperous citizens and the handsome mansions of the princes and boyars.

The oldest Russian towns were Kiev, Chernigov and Novgorod; and in the 10th and 11th centuries Kiev occupied a position of particular importance and, as the capital of the princedom and the place where the Grand Prince held his court, was well named the "mother of Russian cities".

The origin of the name Kiev is unknown, and even the early Russians themselves were unable to decide what it meant. The chronicler, anxious to remain impartial, records two traditions current in his time. The first of these had it that Kiev was named after one Ky, a ferryman on the Dnieper. Alternatively it was thought that the city had been founded by three brothers, the Princes Ky, Shchek and Khoriv, along with their sister the Princess Lybed, and was named after the eldest of the brothers. The memory of the beautiful Princess Lybed is preserved in the placid stream of this name which flows into the Dnieper at Kiev.

Kiev stood on the great water route which ran "from the Varangians to the Greeks"—that is, from the Baltic to the Black Sea—and accordingly it soon developed into an important trading and cultural centre. The hoards of coins found in the Dnieper area bear witness to long-standing commercial relations with Byzantium and the countries of the East, and archaeological discoveries have provided evidence of the flourishing artistic production of the city.

The conversion of Russia to Christianity in the year 988 strengthened the political authority of the Kievan kingdom, for the introduction of a single unitary religion contributed to the rapid unification, "under the right hand of the Grand Prince", of the tribal lands which had hitherto been parcelled out among many owners. Moreover in accepting Christianity Russia became a full member of the family of European nations, able not only to enter into trading agreements with them but to make military and dynastic alliances; and these wider relationships were accompanied by a lively cultural interchange.

The acceptance of the new faith also led to a fundamental change in the character of Russian art. The first stone-built churches decorated with mosaics and frescoes made their appearance, and the art of icon-painting (in tempera on wood, the earliest form of easel-painting in Russia) began to develop.

This flowering of art in the Kievan kingdom took place during the reigns of Prince Vladimir (980-

1015) and Prince Yaroslav the Wise (1019-1054). In this period Kiev's profusion of churches, the sumptuousness of their interiors, and the luxury of the Grand Prince's court impressed not only the half barbarous inhabitants of the steppes but also travellers from other countries who had some experience of the world. Thus Dietmar of Merseburg assures us that he had counted eight market-places and over four hundred churches in Kiev. Even though the latter figure may be somewhat exaggerated, Dietmar's account gives us some idea of the impression produced even on a seasoned traveller by the earliest capital city of Russia.

If by some chance we found ourselves in Kiev as it was at the end of the 10th century and in the 11th, we should certainly lose our way in the densely packed maze of semi-underground huts in which the craftsmen and poorer classes of the town had their dwellings, clustering against the town ramparts and from there extending up the hill in a sea of green turf-covered roofs. Here and there a few timber buildings would stand out from the rest and the domes of churches would soar into the sky, and from place to place the houses would draw aside to make room for a market-place in which the craftsmen's wares and foodstuffs of all kinds were displayed for sale.

On the summit of the hill was the Prince's citadel, the architectural centre of Kiev. Within its walls were a church and the Prince's residence with his private apartments and audience chambers, in which "gracious Prince Vladimir, the Bright Sun" and his knights, raising beakers full of foaming mead, took counsel together on how best to defend the land of Rus against the hordes of the Heathen Idol or the foul serpent Tugarin. All this we learn from the *byliny*, the ancient epic poems of Russia. The chroniclers, too, tell of the Prince's residence with its golden domes and spacious audience chambers. In the square in front of the palace stood a bronze quadriga (four-horse chariot), which Vladimir had brought from Korsun (Chersonesus), and marble statues of goddesses of classical antiquity; and the square accordingly came to be known as the Women's Market.

The Desyatinnaya Church in Kiev was the first stone-built church in Russia. It was the work of Byzantine craftsmen, for Russian builders, being accustomed to working with timber, were not yet skilled in the stone-mason's craft. Moreover it was from Byzantium that Christianity had come to Russia; and it was right, therefore, that the Greeks should teach the newly converted pagans what kind of dwelling was appropriate for the God of the Christians. A rectangular plan, semi-circular or polygonal apses projecting at the eastern end behind the altar, and domes supported on internal piers: this was the pattern of the Byzantine Orthodox church, and it was followed in the Desyatinnaya. But even in this first stone-built church, erected though it was by Greek craftsmen, the influence of Russian taste made itself felt. The church had no fewer than twenty-five domes, a number unheard of in Byzantine architecture. This multiplicity of domes was characteristic of Russian timber churches: the Cathedral of St Sophia in Novgorod *(Plate p. 24)*, for example, built as early as the 10th century—as we learn from the chronicler—had thirteen domes.

When the church was completed in 996, seven years after work had started, Vladimir was so delighted with it that he granted the tenth part of his revenues for its maintenance; and so this church, dedicated to the Dormition of the Virgin, became known as the Desyatinnaya, the Church of the Tithe.

This splendid church, built in the heyday of the Kievan kingdom, did not survive its fall. When the hordes of the Mongol khan Baty or Batu burst into the city in 1240 such of the Kievan forces as

14

survived the battle took refuge in the Desyatinnaya along with a large number of townsfolk. In an attempt to escape they set to digging a tunnel under the church; but the building was unable to withstand the Mongol attacks and collapsed in ruin, burying the defenders under the rubble.

Other buildings dating from Vladimir's reign have likewise failed to survive the centuries. There is more to show for the reign of his successor Yaroslav the Wise, who went in for building in stone, for both military and religious purposes, on a larger scale than his father. Of the churches he built, the largest and most important—not only in Kiev itself but in the whole of Kievan Russia—was the Cathedral of St Sophia (1037 to the middle forties of the 11th century) *(Plates p. 25)*.

As we see it today St Sophia is not particularly impressive, for the additions and reconstructions of the 17th to 19th centuries have transformed the original building beyond recognition. Contemporaries compared it, however, with the splendours of Solomon's temple as described in the Old Testament. As originally built it was a huge structure of severe and noble lines, with its walls patterned in alternate bands of pink and white—for in accordance with Byzantine practice the alternate courses of stone and brick were not plastered over—and with thirteen low domes on polygonal drums. At the east end were five apses, and to the north, west and south were single-storey open arcades. On the west front were two stair-towers giving access to the gallery, which extended as far as the altar and opened into the space under the dome through handsome arches. During the service the Prince's household and court sat at the west end of the gallery, and the doors of the stair-towers were guarded by watchful sentinels, ready to bar the way against any intruder.

The interior of the cathedral was splendidly finished, with its rich mosaics on a gold ground, its frescoes, its flooring of red slate, and its gold and silver vessels gleaming in the light of the countless lamps which illuminated the church.

Most of the mosaics and frescoes have been preserved. (It may be noted that the combination of mosaics and frescoes is a specifically Russian feature: the interiors of Byzantine churches were decorated with either the one or the other but not with both). Particularly fine are the mosaics in the central apse behind the altar which, following the accepted tradition, show the Virgin in the upper part, with a representation of the Liturgical Eucharist (the Communion of the Apostles) below, and—below this again—the Fathers of the Church and other teachers of the Word. The Virgin is represented in the *Orans* pose, raising her arms in the gesture of prayer. She wears a purple tunic with a white kerchief hanging at the waist and a brownish-violet cloak decorated with gold stars round the hem. This figure was popularly known as the "Virgin of the Invulnerable Wall", for the wall containing this mosaic was reputed to be the only one which had survived undamaged the destruction of Kiev by the Mongols. In the Middle Ages, therefore, this image was particularly venerated by the people of Kiev.

When you look at the mosaics in the apse from some distance away, so that the broad dark outlines of the figures are no longer visible, the whole thing seems to come suddenly to life. This effect is due largely to the technique of mosaic-working used. The smalt cubes were not laid in a single plane, as is the modern practice, but at a slight angle to one another, so that light striking the mosaics is refracted at varying angles, creating the impression of a "live", glittering surface.

The frescoes in St Sophia are not all on religious themes. In the north, west and south arcades, for example, were portraits of Yaroslav the Wise, his wife the Princess Irina and their sons and daughters

—the only portraits known in Russian monumental painting of the 11th century. These frescoes are in a poor state of preservation, and our knowledge of the general composition comes from a drawing by the 17th century Dutch artist Abraham van Westerveldt. It is still possible, however, to make out the figures of four princesses, Yaroslav's daughters, ranged one behind the other in order of seniority—which the artist also indicates by making each one slightly smaller than the one before. In front, holding candles, are Elizabeth, later Queen of Norway, and Anne, later the wife of Henry I of France; behind them is Anastasia, who was to become Queen of Hungary; and behind her again is the youngest sister, whose name is not known.

Of particular interest are the paintings in the stair-towers, which are thought to have been commissioned by Yaroslav himself—for the towers were evidently connected by corridors with the Prince's own apartments. These paintings introduce us into the atmosphere of court life—the Imperial court of Byzantium and the princely court of Kiev. They show the famous Hippodrome of Constantinople with the Emperor and Empress and their court sitting in boxes watching boxers, dancers and musicians; entertainers in grotesque masks; and a great variety of animals, often shown in hunting scenes.

The paintings in the towers of St Sophia throw a ray of light on a corner of a long vanished world. We know from various sources, including lives of Russian saints and the *byliny* (folk epics), that the Princes of Kiev, like other princes, were passionately devoted to hunting and were accustomed to while away their leisure hours by watching the antics of various kinds of entertainers and listening to music and singing. The frescoes in St Sophia, however, are the only representations of these themes in the whole of Russian mediaeval painting.

At first sight it may appear strange that such purely secular themes should be represented on the walls of a church. There is no cause for surprise, however, for in the Middle Ages—as we shall have occasion to note again in the course of this book—religious and secular life were so closely bound up together that it is sometimes difficult to determine where the one begins and the other leaves off. This can be illustrated by another example. Until the 15th century there was no public building in Russian towns corresponding to the *rathaus* or town hall of western Europe, and the cathedral would serve in its place. On the upper floor of one of the towers of St Sophia in Kiev was a room in which the Prince held counsel with the boyars and administered justice; and the courtyard of the cathedral and the galleries which opened into it were frequently occupied by a noisy popular assembly, the *Veche*, which discussed matters affecting the interests of the citizenry as a whole.

The citizens of the Russian towns took special pride in their cathedrals. In describing to some stranger the beauties of their native town they would usually begin with the churches; and the Russian chroniclers sometimes identify a particular town by referring to the churches it contains—talking, for example, of "the town with such-and-such a church".

In the first half of the 11th century buildings were erected in stone in many other towns as well as Kiev. Splendid churches were now built, for example, at Chernigov, Polotsk, Pereyaslavl-Yuzhny (Pereyaslavl in the South) and Novgorod. Of these the Cathedral of the Transfiguration in Chernigov was perhaps the most sumptuously adorned church in Kievan Russia after Yaroslav's St Sophia. It was a huge building with five domes and three apses and with a severe exterior, originally finished with alternate bands of stone and brick. On the north and south sides, next the apses, were small chapels which

up into the gallery from the narthex; opposite the staircase is a princely burial vault. A band of ornament resembling the classical meander runs round the top of the external walls.

Even these two examples—and many more could be quoted—are sufficient to demonstrate quite clearly that the experience of building in stone which Russian architects had acquired in the course of the preceding hundred and fifty years had pointed the way towards further creative achievements. Russian building in stone had now broken free from the artistic and other canons of Byzantium and was developing independently.

The type of decoration employed in the churches also changed. Mosaic was used for the last time in the altar of the cathedral in the Mikhaylovsko-Zlatoverkhy Monastery (St Michael with the Golden Roof) in Kiev: thereafter it was replaced by the less expensive and less laborious technique of fresco.

There can be no doubt that numerous icon-painters were at work in Kiev, the capital city of the earliest Russian kingdom. We know the name of Alimpy, who is still referred to in the 13th century as one of "surpassing skill in the painting of icons". Excavation in Kiev has brought to light the remains of an icon-painter's studio, burned down when the Mongols set fire to the city. But not a single icon which can be reliably ascribed to the Kievan school has survived: evidently their whole output was swept away by the Tatar invasion.

Some miniatures painted in books have, however, come down to us; and to some extent at least these replace the missing icons and illuminate certain other aspects of the painting of the 11th and 12th centuries.

The term "miniature" comes from the Latin *minium*, the red colouring matter—cinnabar or red lead—which the old calligraphers used in manuscripts for initial letters and rubrics. The art of miniature painting was known in Russia as early as the first half of the 11th century through the work of Byzantine and Balkan (mainly Bulgarian) artists. At first these foreign models were slavishly copied, but soon a distinct Russian school began to grow up. No doubt we can see one of the causes of its rapid development in the extraordinarily high regard felt in Kievan Russia for books and the "surpassing treasures of wisdom" they contained.

Prince Vladimir sought to establish in Kiev something equivalent to elementary schools, giving orders that "the children of nobles, the middle orders and the needy should be taken and assigned to priests and deacons in divers churches so that they might receive instruction in book learning." Yaroslav the Wise did the same at Novgorod, bringing together in the Cathedral of St Sophia a library which was of outstanding quality by the standards of the day. "Great is our profit from book learning!" cries a contemporary. "From the writings contained in books we gain wisdom and continence. These are the rivers that water the earth; these are the springs of true wisdom."

The books of this period were meticulously and beautifully produced. As in western Europe, they were written by hand on parchment. The text pages were often considerable works of graphic art in their own right, in virtue of the delicacy and beauty of the lettering. This is particularly true of the initial letters, painted in bright colours and often gilded, which were formed from an intricate pattern of scrolls and flourishes interwoven with representations of animals, human heads and other figures. Colouring and gilding were also used in the magnificent headpieces and tailpieces and in the miniatures which were scattered through the book, their themes varying according to the subject-matter of the text.

The colouring used was gouache, which took well on parchment, producing a dense velvety surface. For the groundwork gold leaf, in sheets no thicker than cigarette paper, was used, the leaf being glued to the parchment and then cut round the outline of the design — a costly technique which by the 15th century had been superseded by the use of gold paint. As can be seen, therefore, the methods of book production and of miniature painting were the same as those in use in western Europe at this period.

The oldest and most celebrated examples of the book production of Kievan Russia are the "Ostromir Gospel" (1056; in the Saltykov-Shchedrin Library in Leningrad) and the "Compendium of Svyatoslav" (1073; in the Historical Museum in Moscow). The former was produced by a certain Deacon Gregory for Ostromir, *posadnik* (mayor) of Novgorod, and was illustrated by an unknown miniaturepainter with full-page portraits of the Evangelists *(Plate p. 18)*—following a practice inherited from ancient times of putting the portrait of the author at the beginning of his text. The "Compendium" was made for Prince Izyaslav, son of Yaroslav the Wise, but when Kiev was captured by his brother Svyatoslav the book acquired a new owner and a new title. This splendid manuscript contains four miniatures representing groups of bishops—the authors of the articles included in the collection. Round each group of prelates is an ornamental frame, splendidly gilded, like a schematic representation of a three-domed church, with the figure of a peacock on either side. The peacock, which in antiquity was the constant attendant of Hera-Juno, the goddess of the domestic hearth, came in early Christian and later in mediaeval art to symbolise the Christian church; for it was firmly believed that the peacock's body was incorruptible.

With their bright colouring, their use of gold, and the extraordinary delicacy of their workmanship. the miniatures put us in mind of the jeweller's craft; and in fact the jewellery of this period was of great beauty and was produced in great quantity. Gold and silver rings, bracelets and *kolty* (pendants which hung from women's headdresses over the temples) were richly set with pearls and precious stones; or they might be covered with a lace-like tracery of filigree work or with an intricate pattern of microscopic gold and silver balls, in the technique known as granulation; or they might be richly coated with niello or enamel (a vitreous compound coloured by an admixture of metal oxides).

One of the chief glories of the Kievan artists was their cloisonné enamel work, of a quality scarcely inferior to that produced in Byzantium. It was an intricate technique: on the object to be decorated the design was first scratched out, and the metal within the outline was removed; thin strips of metal were then soldered on to the ground, following the lines of the design, and the spaces between the strips were filled with enamel paste; and the object was then fired, polished after cooling, fired again, and finally burnished. This produced a delicate pattern of colour, an interplay of many hues within which glittered the golden web of the metal framework. The designs covered a wide range, from vegetable ornament to human figures, animals and birds. Perhaps the commonest theme is the bird of ill omen, Sirin—a bird with the head of a beautiful girl, evidently closely related to the sirens of classical Greece, with whose mythology and imagery Kiev was acquainted, not only through Byzantium but through contact with the art of the Greek cities on the Black Sea.

Of equal quality is the niello work, particularly on gold objects. Niello is a compound of various metals and metalloids, most commonly of tin, lead, silver and sulphur. The constituent elements were melted separately and then fused together; and the mixture was then melted

Η СΥΝΑΞΙС ΤΩΝ ΑΓΙωΝ ΔΕΚΑΔΥΟ ΑΠΟΣΤΟΛΩΝ

ΚC ΦΙΛΙΠΠΟC Β̅ РΘ̅
ΜΑ

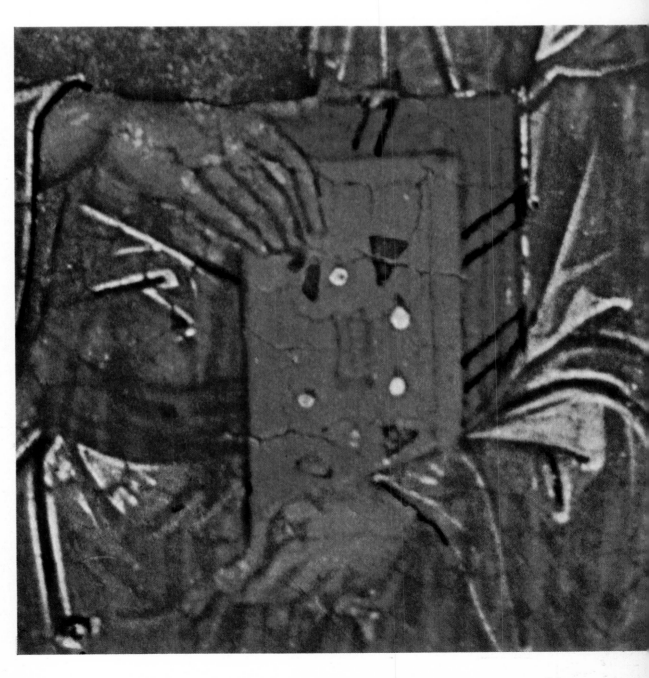

again, allowed to cool, and pounded into a fine powder. At this point the alchemist was transformed into an artist. He took the object to be decorated, which had been got ready for the purpose, cut out the design, sprinkled it with the niello powder and then with borax, and put the whole thing in a kiln on a low fire. Using a wire with a flattened end, he spread out the niello evenly over the appropriate parts of the design during firing. Then, after the final firing, the article was polished and burnished in the same way as the enamel jewellery.

The precious metals were also used for making a variety of articles for both religious and secular use—the bindings of liturgical books, communion vessels, lustres, candlesticks, lavers, wine cups, spoons, and so on. If at a feast given by a prince or a boyar the food and drink were served in anything other than gold or silver vessels this was regarded as a slight on the guests. The warriors of Prince Vladimir's retinue, having been invited by their master to a feast, were gravely offended to find the table set with wooden spoons; whereupon Vladimir, recognising his error, had perforce to acquire silver ones in their place.

The *bogatyrs* of this period also drank their wine from huge aurochs horns set in gold and silver. Two such horns bound with silver were found during the excavation of the "Black Tomb", a funeral *kurgan* erected over the remains of some unknown 10th century warrior not far from Chernigov. On the binding of one of these (now in the Historical Museum in Moscow) is a decoration—partly embossed and partly engraved, with some niello work added—consisting of representations in relief of scaly monsters with intertwined tails, dogs attacking the monsters, a bird wearing a crown, and small running figures of a man and a woman. The man is turning round as he runs to shoot at the bird with his bow. The bird is evidently, however, no ordinary fowl, for the arrows are rebounding from its body and turning back against the archer. It is supposed that the decoration on this horn represents episodes from the *bylina* of Ivan Godinovich. This *bogatyr* won as his wife the Princess Nastasya of Chernigov, who was already the promised bride of Kashchey the Deathless; whereupon Kashchey set out in pursuit, overcame his rival and bound him in chains. Then the birds of ill omen appeared from nowhere, foretelling the doom of the crafty victor. Kashchey the Deathless fired arrow after arrow at them; but in vain, for Ivan Godinovich cast a spell on the arrows so that they returned against the evildoer who had fired them.

The belief in marvels and magic spells prevailed throughout the whole of the Middle Ages, and we need hardly be surprised to find it so active in Kievan Russia. The men of the mediaeval period had their share of very real misfortunes, but in addition they were haunted at every turn, at every step they took, by a host of imaginary terrors. They had only to hear a board creaking in their house, the croak of a raven or the barking of a dog, to cross the path of a monk, to have a bad dream, and at once they wondered what evil these omens might portend. In their fear of the unknown these things often seemed to them more terrifying than war or famine or pestilence, and they sought protection against the forces of evil in the intercession of the saints or—even more readily—in the well-tried remedies of pagan antiquity, the use of amulets and talismans, of magic spells and incantations. A whole century has passed since the conversion of Russia, complains the Metropolitan John, but the ordinary people are still surreptitiously offering sacrifices to Chernobog, the Black God, to the well-spirit and to the water-sprite. With the experience of so many subsequent centuries to go on, however, we know that traces of pagan superstitions survived much longer than the worthy Metropolitan could suspect. For did not peasants living in villages in the Dnieper area in the 19th century still put a nettle plant on the threshold of their houses during what was called Rusala's Week in order to protect themselves from the sly tricks of the water nymphs? And did not the peasants go in search of a flowering fern on Midsummer's Eve? And was there not also the ill-omened Bare Mountain on which, according to a belief long cherished in Kiev, the witches gathered at night to hold their revels, trampling down the grass so that the mountain top became bald and bare? Traditions of this kind were found everywhere, but were particularly common in Kiev—no doubt because in times of remote antiquity this had been one of the great centres of Slav paganism.

All this now belongs to the distant past, and the Kievan kingdom has long vanished from the face of the earth. Its memory still lives, however, in the pages of the chronicles, in the *byliny* and folk tales, in the luminous frescoes of St Sophia, and in the bright colours of the Kievan enamels and miniatures.

III "No City Mightier than Vladimir, no Ruler Mightier than her Prince"

The splitting up of the Kievan kingdom into a number of independent apanages or feudal princedoms led to the development of local schools of art—the schools of Novgorod, Kiev, Vladimir-Suzdal, Galicio-Volhynia, and so on. There were many of these local schools—indeed one for each of the newly established political units from which they take their names. At first the works produced by the various schools—particularly in the field of painting—showed no very significant differences; but as time went on the artistic ideals of Byzantium receded into the background and local preferences and distinctive local identities began to assert themselves ever more strongly. The architecture of the princedom of Vladimir-Suzdal in the 12th century, for example, is so individual that it can be distinguished at once from the architecture of Chernigov, Novgorod, Smolensk or other Russian towns; and among the monuments of the pre-Mongol period the churches of Vladimir-Suzdal stand out as the most beautiful and most magnificent. This splendour is found not only in their interiors, which have the same sumptuousness as St Sophia in Kiev or the Cathedral of the Saviour in Chernigov, but extends also to their external architecture, which is of princely magnificence. The reason for this is clear: in the 12th century, with the decline of the Princedom of Kiev, there was developing in north-eastern Russia a second Russian kingdom with its capital at Vladimir.

The rise of Vladimir began at the end of the 11th century, when the area fell by right of inheritance to Vladimir Monomakh. Having thereupon come into conflict with Prince Oleg of Chernigov, Vladimir felt the need of a secure fortress—for he could have little reliance on the old-established towns in this area, Rostov and Suzdal. Accordingly, on the high bank of the River Klyazma, on the hills which commanded the road from Ryazan and Murom, he caused a ring of earthen ramparts to be constructed, surmounted by stout oak palisades and surrounded by deep ditches which linked the ends of natural ravines. Within these defences were the Prince's *terem* (tower or keep) and the residences of his boyars, along with various store-rooms and domestic offices; and, as was proper, there soared above these secular buildings the radiant golden dome of the Church of the Saviour, the first stone church to be built in this area. And so there came into being the town of Vladimir, baptised by its founder with his own name.

Vladimir's son Yury, known as Dolgoruky ("Long Arms"), established his capital in the old city of Suzdal and showed little interest in his father's creation. Nor indeed did he spend much time in this or any other city, for his whole life was spent in expeditions to the south, dreaming of the throne of the Kievan kingdom, until at last he died ingloriously by drinking poisoned wine at the very moment when his object seemed to have been achieved. Two buildings dating from the time of Yury Dolgoruky have survived in north-eastern Russia—the Cathedral of the Saviour in Pereyaslavl-Zalessky, a severe structure with massive walls and a single dome, and the Church of SS. Boris and Gleb in the princely village of Kideksha, now almost unrecognisable under the reconstructions carried out in later periods.

The golden age of the princedom of Vladimir-Suzdal and of its art came in the reigns of Yury's sons, Andrey (1157-1175) and Vsevolod III (1177-1212). The latter was the father of a large family, which earned him the name of "Big Brood".

Having taken part in many of his father's campaigns against Kiev, Prince Andrey realised clearly the fruitlessness of Yury's aspirations. His own ambitions lay elsewhere: his dream was to establish in north-eastern Russia a powerful new kingdom with Vladimir as its capital. His choice of Vladimir was no accident: he saw the advantages of its convenient situation, the surrounding forests which served as a defence and also provided a supply of building material, and the abundance of water, so essential in the event of a long siege and so favourable to the development of trade. The nearby Volga played the same part in the economy of this area as the Dnieper in the areas to the south. Finally there was one other important factor in the choice of Vladimir. The population of the town consisted mainly of craftsmen, small traders and peasants, who were in feudal vassalage to the boyars of Rostov; and it was in these classes that Andrey hoped to find support against the old noble families of Rostov and Suzdal, among whom his ambitious plans had provoked a storm of protest.

An alliance between Prince and townsfolk was a common phenomenon in the feudal world, and was usually successful, at least for a period. At any rate Andrey's political calculations turned out to be correct: the boyars' resistance was broken, apparently for good. Now the Prince was able to devote himself to the embellishment of his new capital, which was to bear witness to the success of his plans and accordingly must outshine all the other cities of Russia.

Ceaselessly throughout the day and night, therefore, carts laden with white limestone rolled from the quarries of the lower Oka valley to the hill of Vladimir. Great numbers of craftsmen were employed —summoned, as the chronicler tells us, "from every corner of the earth". Among them were heard the abrupt accent of the north Russians, the melodious speech of the south, and even dialects from some countries of western Europe. There was nothing unusual about this, for in the Middle Ages groups of masons, painters and other craftsmen were accustomed to travel from place to place and from country to country, offering their services to any who stood in need of them.

Under Andrey's impulsion the town of Vladimir, which in the reign of Yury Dolgoruky had been scarcely more than a huddle of mean houses, changed beyond recognition in the short space of some seven or eight years. By the year 1165 the lower slopes of the hill of Vladimir were resounding with the constant noise and bustle of the traders' and craftsmen's quarter. Vladimir Monomakh's cave town on the hill was ringed with new fortifications, and in its southern corner rose a church of outstanding beauty, the Cathedral of the Dormition. Its walls, dazzlingly white in the sun, and its helm-shaped golden dome with the cross standing out against the sky were visible for a distance of many miles. Beside the old town of Vladimir Monomakh stood the "New Town" with its two churches—which themselves were not new—and the newly built mansions of the Prince and his favourites. It was entered by four gateways. The principal entrance, which was on the west side, as in Kiev, was called the Golden Gate (no doubt because the massive oak doors were bound with gilded bronze). Above the entrance stood the Church of the Laying On of the Virgin's Veil. In front of the Golden Gate the townsfolk swore allegiance to their Prince, and also greeted the visitors from distant places who were always welcome to the city. The Volga Gate on the south side of the town gave access to the landing-place on

the River Klyazma, where vessels belonging to Vladimir and to other cities on distant shores, laden with cargoes of goods, swayed gently by the wharf amid the creaking of anchor chains.

Of all these structures—the walls, the palaces and the churches—nothing remains today but the Golden Gate and the Cathedral of the Dormition. Of the original gateway, indeed, only the main arch is left: all the rest of the present structure dates from the 18th century. Nor is the Cathedral as we see it today the original structure; but its rebuilding took place in the same century in which it was built, between 1185 and 1189. It still stands today as it stood then—a massive building with five domes, majestic splayed doorways, and narrow slits of windows in deep embrasures which are also framed in a series of receding arches. Half way up the walls is a band of blind arcades, and there are similar arcades round the top of the apse walls. Above the windows are occasional sculptured mascarons The original cathedral built by Prince Andrey was of rather smaller dimensions, with a single dome and two towers with gilded tent roofs on the west front; but it, too, had bands of blind arcades, the spaces between the colonnettes being decorated with painted figures of peacocks and saints. In the reconstruction and enlargement of the cathedral in 1185-1189 arched openings were made in these walls, which were now inside the walls of the new building. Only a few fragments of the 12th century paintings in the Cathedral have been preserved; the rest of the paintings now visible were done in the early years of the 15th century, when the artists included the famous Andrey Rublëv.

On 28th August, the feast of the Dormition of the Mother of God, enormous numbers of people flocked to Vladimir from all over Russia. Two cords were drawn through the crowd, beginning inside the church and stretching across the Cathedral Square to the Bishop's Palace, and on these cords were hung gold-brocaded ecclesiastical vestments, richly adorned with pearls and precious stones. The immense crowd gazed with bated breath as these splendid fabrics fluttered in the breeze, in a shimmer of gold and an interplay of vivid hues. Then between these gorgeous walls. which seemed almost alive in their rich colouring and constant movement, an endless queue of people—subdued and silent, almost overwhelmed by the luxury which surrounded them—made their way into the church. The fame of this splendid cathedral, and of the fabulous wealth of the northern ruler who had built it, spread far and wide, multiplied a hundredfold by popular report.

Why, it may be asked, did these pious pilgrims flock to Vladimir on the feast of the Dormition?

Having demonstrated by force of arms the superiority of his new northern capital to the older capital in the south, Prince Andrey was concerned to make Vladimir a centre not only of the political but also of the spiritual life of the country. This position had previously been occupied by Kiev, at least in religious matters; for Kiev contained the residence of the Metropolitan, the famous Pechersky Monastery with the caves in which the earliest holy men of Kiev were buried, and many churches in which were treasured some of the most ancient and most revered objects of worship in Russia. In his concern to cast off the spiritual suzerainty of Kiev, and by the same token to free himself from that of Byzantium, Andrey himself appointed the Bishop of Vladimir—though hitherto all bishops had had to be confirmed by the Metropolitan of Kiev—and established the cult of local miracle-workers. In addition he brought from Kiev the famous icon of the Mother of God, the Virgin of Vladimir which was one of the most hallowed objects of mediaeval Russia and is now in the Tretyakov Gallery *(Plate p. 36).*

The Virgin of Vladimir is represented in the pose known as "Our Lady's Tenderness". She is shown at half length, her head bent over the infant whom she holds in her right arm. The compressed lips, the hint of a frown, the expression of profound anguish in her dark eyes create an extraordinarily expressive image of a mother oppressed by the foreboding of evil to come. The child presses his cheek to her face; one of his arms is round her neck, the other clutches her stole. In this convulsive movement and in the upturned glance with which he seeks his mother's eye we divine a momentary impulse of fright and an unspoken plea for help. The unknown Byzantine master of the late 11th or early 12th century has expressed in this icon, with tremendous force, the whole profundity of wordless human suffering. The Virgin's face is painted with outstanding skill. The pink colouring of her cheeks seems to flow from within the dark golden brown of her skin. The translucent olive shadows give tenderness to the lines of the face and, clustering more thickly under the eyes, strengthen the expression of tragic sorrow. The only highlight is provided by a touch of scarlet on the lips. The infant's face is painted in brighter colours and the shadows are even more translucent—no doubt in an attempt to convey the particular colouring of childhood.

It was probably this perfection of artistry that gave rise to the legend that the icon was the work of St Luke himself, the patron saint of painters. Moreover it had the reputation throughout Russia of being a wonder-working icon, and pilgrims oppressed by the troubles and sorrows of this world came from far and wide to worship it. Thus when this widely revered icon was set up in the Cathedral of the Dormition the Mother of God became the patron of the city of Vladimir and of the Princes of Vladimir, sanctifying all their actions with the prestige of her name, and the icon itself became known as the "Virgin of Vladimir".

Andrey built two other churches in honour of his heavenly patron. The first of these is the Church of the Protection of the Virgin on the River Nerl, the leading building in the monastery of the same name which then occupied the site (Plate p. 40, right).

The feast of the Protection of the Virgin is a purely Russian celebration which was introduced at this period. The legend of the Protection (i.e., the Virgin's veil) is of Byzantine origin. The story goes that the blessed Andrey Yurodivy (Andrew the Simple), while praying with a disciple in the famous Church of the Blachernae, saw the Mother of God standing in the principal doorway of the church. Unseen to any others, she went up to the altar and spread her veil over the worshippers, as if promising her intercession in any sorrow or misfortune. The Mother of God was represented in this pose in the icons of the Protection of the Virgin which from the 14th century onwards appeared throughout Russia in increasing numbers. The first church built in honour of the Protection of the Virgin was the one on the Nerl (1165).

The site selected for the monastery was subject to flooding by the Klyazma and the Nerl in spring; and to meet this difficulty the builders first erected an artificial mound, facing it with fair white stone and providing channels for rainwater to run off, and only then began the construction of their church.

The mound is now covered by many centuries' deposit of soil, burying its stone facing and changing its shape. Nothing is now visible of the monastic buildings, or of the splendid stone arcade which once surrounded the church. But the church itself still stands as it has stood for eight centuries, gracefully mirrored in the waters of the River Nerl, which is now much silted up. This is undoubtedly the most beautiful and most graceful of the old Russian churches. It is quite small, with a single dome and narrow apses projecting only a short distance from the nave. The soaring upward movement and the delicate and harmonious lines are accentuated by the slender pilasters which give proportion to the walls, the tall narrow windows, and the blind arcades with rather elongated colonnettes which run round the building. The effect is still further enhanced by the beautiful splayed doorways richly decorated with carving, the sculptured mascarons, and the griffins and figures of Biblical characters above the windows and in the *zakomary* (the rounded gable heads).

The year 1165, in which the Church of the Protection was finished, also saw the completion of the nearby palace of Bogolyubovo. The name indicates that this was the dwelling-place of God-fearing people ; but the actual story of Bogolyubovo has little enough connection with God. The boyars of Rostov and Suzdal, who had resisted the absolutist policy of the Grand Prince, had been forced into outward compliance but had by no means lost hope of securing their revenge ; and since a rebellion of the great feudal lords might flare up whenever a favourable opportunity occurred it was essential to maintain a vigilant watch on Rostov and Suzdal. The Prince therefore needed a powerful fortress on the road between Suzdal and Vladimir which should serve as a constantly manned strong point and watching post. In order that the building might be completed without delay or hindrance Andrey sought the help of his heavenly patroness. In the "Account of the Wonders Wrought by the Icon of Our Lady of Vladimir" we are told, among other marvels, that when the icon was brought from Kiev the horses halted at the exact place where the Prince had in mind to build his fortress, and could not be persuaded to move from the spot. This "wonder" was, of course, interpreted as meaning that the Mother of God desired that a church should be built in her honour on this site. Where a church was to be built it was reasonable to build a palace ; and in those days a palace must necessarily be fortified. And so the palace of Bogolyubovo was built, and Prince Andrey became known as Bogolyubsky, the man who loved God.

All that now remains of the great complex of 12th century buildings—the palace itself, the Church of the Nativity of Our Lady, and various domestic and military structures—is the lower part of the north tower, handsomely built in stone, the passage leading from the tower into the gallery of the church, and part of the adjacent north wall of the church. The rest of the structure dates from the 17th to 19th centuries. Fragments which have survived show that the palaces of the princedom of Vladimir-Suzdal presented the same architectural features as the churches of this area, including the use of stone and the decoration of the external walls with blind arcades.

After Andrey Bogolyubsky's death in 1175—tradition had it that he was killed in the north tower of his palace, the one still visible today—all that he had achieved seemed doomed to destruction. His death led to a rising of the people of Bogolyubovo and the citizens of Vladimir, who were devoted to his cause ; and when this had been quelled the quarrels of the feudal lords flared up once again. This continued for two years until Andrey's brother Vsevolod, "Big Brood", became Grand Prince and, after carrying out savage reprisals, set about restoring order in all the apanages of the princedom. He had the advantage of a well-trained army, so numerous that —in the picturesque language of the "Lay of Igor's Raid"—the Prince's warriors might have emptied the Don with their helmets and spilled the Volga with their oars ; and he also pursued a successful foreign policy, achieved military victory, and maintained wide-ranging trading and cultural relations with the countries of the West and with Byzantium. In short, the twenty-five years of Vsevolod's reign were the most brilliant period in the history of the princedom of Vladimir. Throughout these years much building was done, and a local chronicler records that, unlike Andrey, Vsevolod no longer found it necessary to "look to the *nemtsy* (Germans)[1] for his craftsmen." Among the buildings now erected were a number of monasteries and churches and the Prince's palace in Vladimir. The only part of the palace which survives is the Cathedral of St Dmitry (Demetrius), which—like the church in Bogolyubovo—seems to have been directly connected with the palace.

At first glance the Cathedral of St Dmitry *(Plate p. 39)*, built between 1193 and 1197, resembles the churches of Andrey Bogolyubsky's reign. Like them, it was single-domed, with a vaulted roof, the same articulation of the external walls and the same splayed doorways, slit-like windows and blind arcades. Sculptured decoration, however, which was only sparingly employed in Andrey's buildings, now develops into a riot of ornament. An interwoven pattern of leaves and ribbons fills the spaces between the windows in the drum under the dome, and extends to the arches, the cornices, and the colonnettes and capitals of the blind arcades. The whole of the upper part of the walls is covered with carved representations of a multitude of fabulous creatures, stylised plants, galloping horsemen and saints; and other figures of saints are fitted in between the colonnettes of the blind arcades.

Apart from some scenes with an identifiable content—Vsevolod with a child in his lap and his sons kneeling in front of him, the Baptism of Christ, the Ascension of Alexander, and one or two others—the significance of these reliefs presents us with a puzzle which scholars have been unable to solve: none of the suggestions put forward so far seems plausible. Perhaps, however, there is no point in seeking to interpret them: their main interest lies elsewhere. For surely these sirens and hippogriffs, these lions with human faces and tails in the form of vegetable tendrils, and all the other fantastic images conceived by the fertile imagination of the ancient pagans are quite out of place on the walls of a Christian church? Their appearance in Vladimir, however, is not fortuitous. In this area Christianity was introduced later than in the territory of Kiev, and had difficulty in establishing itself. Even in the early 12th century there were many who remained faithful to the ancient gods. Luxuriant patterns of pagan ornament were woven into the fabric of the Christian legends, and vestiges of pagan conceptions can frequently be detected in Christian art. If we remember that the Cathedral of St Dmitry was built and decorated by local craftsmen we need not be surprised by the type of ornament they preferred; nor is it surprising that the Church authorities were displeased. In public no one dared to run counter to the "ambitious Prince of Vladimir", as he was called; but the Bishop's chronicler, enumerating all the buildings erected by Vsevolod, made no mention of the most grandiose and magnificent of them all, treating the Cathedral of St Dmitry as if it had vanished from the face of the earth.

The cathedral contains fragments of a 12th century painting of the Last Judgment *(Plate p. 38)*, showing St Peter leading a procession of the righteous into Paradise, in which we see the Mother of

---

[1] In mediaeval Russia the word *nemtsy* (Germans) was applied to all foreigners, whatever their nationality, The Russian word is connected with the adjective *nemoy,* meaning "dumb" – i.e., one who could not speak Russian.

God, the patriarchs Abraham, Isaac and Jacob, and the twelve Apostles seated on golden thrones, with angels behind them. Some parts of the painting are very fine, others are of poorer quality. Clearly a number of different hands are at work; and we know from other sources that on large commissions many different craftsmen were employed.

The Cathedral of St Dmitry was the last great achievement of the architecture of Vladimir. Building work continued until Vsevolod's death in 1212, under the impulsion of the Prince himself, the Princess his wife, and John, Bishop of Vladimir; but the character of the architecture changed. It became less exuberant, more austere; brick was used as well as stone, and the sculptured ornament disappeared from the walls of the churches.

After Vsevolod's death the bloody rivalries between the feudal lords were renewed. The unified Russian state, created at the cost of so much effort, began to break up into fragments. Vladimir ceased to be the capital, and its artistic life gradually died out as its craftsmen went off to other feudal centres in quest of employment. There was no shortage of work in these other towns, but the development of their art followed a rather different pattern from that of Vladimir. And of course time was moving on: it was now the second quarter of the 13th century, and tastes were showing a distinct change.

Of these later buildings, perhaps the closest in style to the 12th century churches in Vladimir are the Cathedral of the Nativity of the Virgin in Suzdal and the Cathedral of St George in Yuryev-Polsky[1].

The Cathedral of the Nativity *(Plate p. 40 above left)* was originally built by Vladimir Monomakh at the turn of the 11th and 12th centuries. The use of brick indicates that it was the work of craftsmen from Kiev, no doubt brought by Vladimir when he came to take over his princedom. Between 1222 and 1225 it was thought necessary for some reason—perhaps because the exterior of the original church was too plain for contemporary taste—to reconstruct it. The brick walls were torn down and rebuilt in tufa, and the architectural details—the slender pilasters which articulate the external walls, the carved doorways, the colonnettes on the apses and the blind arcades—were also of stone. The decorative effect was achieved by the contrast between the finely dressed stone detailing and the irregular porous texture of the grey stone in which the walls were built, so that the details stand out sharply against the darker background.

The present church is very different from its 13th century appearance. Like most old buildings, it was frequently rebuilt and added to in later centuries. In the 1950s and early 1960s a number of later additions in brick were cleared away; but the only part of the 13th century building which still survives is the lower part of the walls, including the blind arcades.

The church contains some remains of ancient paintings (1233). In the upper part of the southern apse, for example, are the figure of two saintly old men with the austere and emaciated faces of ascetics *(Plate p. 45)*. Most of the painting, however, consists of geometric and vegetable ornament. A stylised pattern of intertwining plants also decorates the walls of the niches under the gallery, in the burial vault of the Princes and Bishops of Suzdal.

---

[1] "Polsky" does not mean Polish, as might be thought, but comes from *pole,* a field: the town stood amid fields.

Other features from the same period which have survived are the double doors in the west and south doorways. These are clad with bronze and decorated with engravings of Biblical scenes and various saints, intricately damascened in gold.

The Cathedral of the Nativity was rebuilt by Prince George, son of Vsevolod "Big Brood", with whom the reader is already acquainted. The Cathedral of St George in Yuryev-Polsky, however, is associated with another of Vsevolod's sons, Svyatoslav.

Yuryev-Polsky, then the principal city of Svyatoslav's apanage, had since 1152 possessed a small and modest church dedicated to St George the Victorious. The builders of this church seem to have been poor workmen, or perhaps they were working with poor material: at any rate the church soon began to show signs of dilapidation, and by the third decade of the following century stood in urgent need of repair. But Svyatoslav would not hear of repairing the unassuming old building, which seemed an affront to his dignity as a Prince. In 1230, therefore, the church was demolished, and within three years there arose in its place a fine new church built entirely of fair white stone, like the churches of Vladimir. But none of the churches in Vladimir—not even St Dmitry—was so lavishly adorned with carved ornament. The carvings covered the whole surface of the walls and doorways, from the ground upwards, as if the craftsmen who built the church were afraid of leaving any corner without ornament. And what a variety of subject matter is represented in these carvings! From the blind arcades the stone images of saints look down with unseeing eyes, and the walls, colonnettes and doorway arches are covered with a riot of vegetable ornament, enfolding in its coils a variety of human figures and animals and birds. The eye can scarcely follow the endlessly changing pattern; nor is it easy to distinguish in this confusion of themes any over-all scheme of decoration or any controlling idea behind the profusion of ornament. This is because the Cathedral of St George as it now exists belongs to two different periods, the 13th and the 15th centuries. In the 15th century the roof of the church collapsed, carrying with it the upper part of the walls, and in 1471 the Grand Prince of Moscow, Ivan III, sent the famous Moscow builder and sculptor, Vasily Ermolin, to repair it. It cannot be said, however, that the rebuilding of St George's was one of his most successful achievements. The walls as he rebuilt them were too low, so that the band of blind arcades came almost immediately under the roof and the building as a whole was of rather squat and clumsy proportions. Moreover Ermolin had apparently neither the time nor the patience to work out the pattern of the original carved ornament, and in many cases the arrangement of the stones was determined largely by their size. The result was like a child's jigsaw in which all the pieces were fitted into place but the pattern was lost.

Like other early Russian churches, the cathedrals of Vladimir-Suzdal were originally decorated with paintings; but unfortunately only a few of them have preserved any of these paintings, and then only in the form of fragments. We are still worse off in relation to the icons of this period. We have a small group of icons which are attributed to the Vladimir-Suzdal (or Rostov-Suzdal) school *(Plate p. 46)*, partly on account of their provenance, partly on the basis of stylistic comparison with, for example, the frescoes in St Dmitry. The trouble is that the icons of the 12th and early 13th centuries, no matter from what part of Russia they come, mostly express the general style of the period, and it is a matter of extreme difficulty to identify distinctive local features. The only icon which we can say with confidence was painted in Vladimir, and nowhere else, is the Virgin of Bogolyubovo; but this icon is in such a state of ruin that it cannot be used as a basis of stylistic comparison.

The situation is very different with the art of the silversmith and the goldsmith, where we find distinct differences in local styles. These crafts were no less developed in this area than in the territory of Kiev. The princes and boyars wore garments decorated with patterned gold and silver plaques, garnished with coloured silks, brocaded with metal threads and set with pearls and precious stones. Their wives wore headdresses from which hung strings of jingling pendants, and costly rings glittering in all the colours of the rainbow. The warriors' armour and weapons were adorned with gold and silver, and at their feasts food and drink were served in gold and silver vessels. All this was part of the way of life of noble families in this period, not only in Russia but in other countries: the surprising and characteristic feature, however, is that at the sight of any of the articles produced by the local jewellers we are at once reminded of the churches of Vladimir. This is natural enough, of course, in the case of objects serving a liturgical use—for example reliquaries, tabernacles and censers, which are often in the form of churches with one or more domes—particularly in the mediaeval period but also in later centuries. But we find the same thing in objects not merely of a secular but of a frivolous nature—in articles of personal adornment, for example.

Among the commonest of such articles are *naruchi*, a kind of broad bracelet or bangle used to gather the sleeves of under garments at the wrist. They are in two halves, which are joined by long hinges, and are made of silver embossed with relief ornament, sometimes with the addition of niello but usually with a rich coating of gilt. (We may remark in passing that whereas the Kievans liked the combination of niello and enamel with gold the citizens of Vladimir preferred the use of gold on silver). Each half of the bracelet had a raised rim, either plain or ornamented, and there was sometimes also an embossed ridge running across the middle—producing something of the same effect as the cornices and pilasters which were used to break up the walls of churches. The rest of the surface is usually divided into separate panels by embossed gilt colonnettes and arches. In these golden cages are contained all manner of fierce creatures—snarling lions with birds' legs, lashing their tails in impotent fury at winged monsters which seem to have descended from the walls of St Dmitry's or St George's at the behest of some magician. Sometimes, too, there are human figures; but the commonest figure of all is the griffin. This fantastic creature, a cross between a bird and a beast of prey, had been a favourite decorative theme on gold and silver objects from time immemorial. The ancient Greeks had called the griffin the "guardian of treasure" and had used it as a decoration on the doors of the royal treasuries; and it had the same significance in the thought of the mediaeval world. It is of interest to note that these bracelets, like most of the jewellery we possess dating from the late 12th and the 13th centuries, were found in hoards or "treasures". It must be added, however, that the representations of griffins guarded the valuables entrusted to their care not by inspiring terror but by appealing to conscience—and with some success, for the famous Treasure of Vladimir lay undisturbed in the ground for six and a half centuries before being discovered in 1896.

But these fabulous creatures, so fantastically combined with human figures and even with representations of saints, are not the only reminiscence of church art and architecture; for do not these tiny gilded arches on their silver background remind us of the gilded arcades standing out against the plain white surface of the cathedral walls? Evidently the churches of Vladimir, combining severe architectural form with a riot of carved ornament, had made a powerful impression on the contemporary imagination.

As we survey the art of Vladimir we are inevitably struck by the contrast between the magnitude of its achievement and the brief period of its flowering. For by the end of the first quarter of the 13th century the kingdom of the Grand Princes of Vladimir, lately so powerful, was weltering in blood and ravaged by interminable fratricidal wars. And while these troubles were at their height came the first intimations of a greater catastrophe. The teeming Mongol hordes from the steppes of Asia advanced on the land of Rus, leaving a wake of smoking ruins and mountains of corpses wherever they passed. In February 1238 they reached Vladimir. The citizens resisted heroically, although they realised that this was the beginning of the end: an end that was hastened by the fatal circumstance that there had not been time to rebuild the old timber west gate of the city, the Klyazma Gate, in stone. To make matters worse, the besieging army managed to break through the walls near the Church of the Saviour. The city was captured, plundered and set on fire, and the inhabitants were put to the sword. The Cathedral of the Dormition was burned down, and in the fire perished the Bishop of Vladimir and the family of George, son of Vsevolod, last Prince of Vladimir, who had taken refuge in the gallery of the church.

The princedom of Vladimir-Suzdal now disappeared from history, but the artistic traditions which had developed here were not destined to die. We shall find them renewing themselves and coming to fresh flowering in a new soil, in the architecture of Moscow under its Grand Princes.

IV   Lord Novgorod the Great and his Younger Brother Pskov

In the history of mediaeval Russia Novgorod occupies a position of exceptional importance, and no account of the artistic culture of the period can be complete if it neglects the art of Novgorod. Conversely, the art of Novgorod cannot be fully understood without some knowledge, even in the most general terms, of certain features of the historical development of the city; for though in many ways it resembles the history of other Russian cities it also shows a number of features peculiar to itself.

The basis of Novgorod's prosperity was trade, the rapid development of which was promoted by the abundance of lakes and rivers in the area, and above all by the proximity of the sea. None of the cities of ancient Rus extended its trading relations so widely as Novgorod, which had dealings with almost the whole known world. The great water route "from the Varangians to the Greeks" passed through Novgorod, and to Novgorod came vessels from Byzantium, Sweden, Denmark and —from the 14th century onwards—the cities of the Hanseatic League. The shops of Novgorod sold not only local products but fabrics and precious objects from the East, spices and wine from distant lands; and in return the amber-yellow wax of Novgorod and splendid furs from the northern countries found a ready market in Byzantium, Italy and France.

The development of trade and of craft industry always go hand in hand. Novgorod was no exception to the rule: it was a city not only of merchants but of skilled craftsmen. There were so many of them that many streets, and even whole districts of the city, were named after the various trades; and archaeological excavation has recovered the objects they produced in stone, metal, wood or bone—furniture, dishes and utensils, weapons, footwear, snow-shoes, chessmen and many other articles—in great quantity and variety.

Novgorod's accumulation of wealth and wide-ranging connections with the whole of the civilised world of the day led to a rapid spiritual development and a rapid growth of art and culture, in particular the art of building. It is noteworthy, too, that the whole population of the city—from the Prince and the Archbishop to the least of the townsfolk—were involved in this building activity in one way or another.

"Lord Novgorod the Great": by this title the city was known throughout the land of Rus. Why, we may ask, was this honour not paid to Kiev, or Vladimir, or any other city? The essential difference was that Novgorod recognised no other lord and master than itself: it was the first republic of the mediaeval period in Russia. The Princes ruled as sovereigns of Novgorod only until the thirties of the 12th century: thereafter they were merely military commanders whose actions were subject to the control of the popular assembly, the *Veche*. If a Prince broke his agreement with the *Veche* he was dismissed, and someone else took his place; and the *Veche* maintained a similar control over other elected dignitaries. It is true that in the 14th century the boyars, led by the Mayor and the Archbishop, succeeded in gaining mastery of the popular assembly; but even at this period the common people were sometimes able to regain control of the *Veche*. Sometimes, also, two rival assemblies met at the same time; and this commonly led to the destruction of a few boyars' mansions, a hand-to-hand fight on the bridge over the Volkhov or, at the very least, a street brawl. Risings of the townspeople were also of frequent occurrence: between the middle of the 12th century and the end of the 15th there were more than eighty.

In short, life in Novgorod was freer than in other mediaeval Russian cities. It was no accident that the first Russian heresies developed here. Nor is it unexpected to find one of the favourite heroes of the Novgorod *byliny*, Vaska Buslaev, proclaiming that he has faith neither in dreams, nor in sneezes, nor in the croaking of ravens, nor in any other portents, but only in his own valour and daring—an independence of mind which is unprecedented in the feudal world.

The art of Novgorod reflects not only certain specific features of the city's historical development and of its social and political life but also the practical, matter-of-fact cast of mind of the citizens of mediaeval Novgorod. The architecture of Novgorod, for example, is not given to magnificence or elegant refinement; and the figures which look down on us from the icons are usually those of the pation saints of commerce and the various crafts, and of the different aspects of economic life. In short the art of mediaeval Novgorod is closely related to the needs of everyday life and the daily concerns of the citizens.

For us who live in the 20th century the artistic culture of Novgorod has a particular interest. During the terrible years of the *Tatarshchina*, when the land was red with the glow of fires and once-flourishing cities lay in shapeless heaps of rubble, the artistic life of Russia was almost completely wiped out. Here and there, perhaps, a spark still smouldered under the ashes—no more than smouldered, for in those days men were mainly concerned about the roof over their heads, their daily bread, and the good sword they wielded. Only in Novgorod was it otherwise. The dense forests which surrounded the city, and the network of swamps, rivers and streams which flooded the countryside in the spring spates, provided an almost impregnable defence against the Tatars, Novgorod's artistic development was hampered but not brought to a halt by the onslaught of Baty and his Mongols. For our knowledge of Russian art in the 13th and even the 14th century, therefore, we must depend mainly on the work produced in Novgorod, which has come down to us in incomparably greater quantity than the arts of other parts of Russia, and has accordingly been the subject of much more intensive study. Novgorod, the "new city", is in fact one of the oldest cities in Russia; almost as old as Kiev. No doubt it was given this name by comparison with the older fortified settlement established by the Slavs of the Lake Ilmen area.

By the 12th century Novgorod was a bustling commercial town which had spread to both banks of the Volkhov. The left bank, with the *kreml* or citadel and the Cathedral of St Sophia, was known as the "St Sophia Quarter"; the right bank, with the market and the square in which the *Veche* met, as the "Commercial Quarter". The two parts of the town were linked by a timber bridge over the Volkhov.

Unlike the cities of Kievan Rus and Vladimir-Suzdal—which were a confused huddle of stone and timber buildings, mud huts and semi-underground houses—Novgorod was mainly built of timber. The only stone structures were the walls and towers which protected the city from attack and the many churches; but these isolated stone buildings were lost in a sea of timber houses. Of timber, too—as we learn from a local chronicler—was the first Christian church built in the town, the Church of St Sophia (989), of which no trace has survived.

Novgorod was—by the standards of the time, at least—well provided with amenities. It had, for example, a water supply system of a rather primitive kind; excavation has shown that as early as the 10th century timber paving was beginning to appear; and by the 11th century all the streets were paved. The *Yaroslavova Pravda*, the first written code of Russian law, refers to the "roadmaking duty" as obligatory for all: the Prince was required to pave a given stretch of road, the Archbishop was responsible for another, and similarly with the boyars, the merchants, and even foreigners resident in the town.

The wide, level streets were lined with solid timber houses roofed with boarding, often of two stories. The ground floor or basement was not heated and served as a store-room. The houses were set back from the street behind a paling, and to the rear were timber-paved courtyards with various domestic offices.

The streets of Novgorod were filled all day long with noisy, bustling life. This activity began very early in the morning: at six o'clock the bells of the countless churches sounded the call to matins, the shutters of the shopkeepers' booths and the warehouses were thrown open, and the first wisps of smoke began to curl into the air above the houses. To the chimes of the bells were added the clang of the blacksmiths' hammers, the screeching of saws, the rumble of carts and the voices of the shopkeepers crying their wares. As the day wore on the streets and the market-place were filled with a ceaseless flow of people—thrifty housewives hurrying to buy provisions from the hawkers' trays, foreign visitors vainly trying to explain something to a craftsman much the worse for liquor, peasants walking with unhurried step alongside their carts. Then suddenly there would resound urgently through the town the rapid tolling of a bell and, abandoning at once whatever they were doing, the citizens would pour through the streets to the Assembly Square. This square, in the Commercial Quarter, had once been occupied by the palace of Yaroslav the Wise (the memory of which is preserved in the Scandinavian sagas). By the middle of the 12th century the site of the palace was occupied by the Assembly Bell and the rostrum from which the *posadnik* (mayor) and the military leaders of Novgorod addressed the citizens, and on which the Princes kissed a cross and swore allegiance to Lord Novgorod the Great.

On feast days a great silence settled on the city, broken only by the pealing of the bells as the people of Novgorod walked sedately to the city's many churches. Of these the largest and the oldest was the Cathedral of St Sophia, built by Prince Vladimir, son of Yaroslav, between 1045 and 1050. The name of the cathedral and the fact that it stood in the *kreml* suggest that its builders were seeking to imitate the architecture of Kiev under its Grand Princes; but this was not in fact the case. The cathedral is built in roughly dressed local stone with a small amount of brick, and has five domes, with a sixth over the stair-tower. The arrangement of large masses, the small number of windows and the absence of any ornament on the walls combine with the considerable dimensions of the cathedra to create an impression of austerity and dignified simplicity.

The style of the interior matched that of the exterior. It was simple, severe, and quite lacking in the luxuriant ornament found in the Cathedral of St Sophia in Kiev. Mosaic decoration, for example, was employed only in the central apse and in the flooring. For some unknown reason the church was not painted until the 12th century: the work is referred to by the chronicler in the years 1108 and 1144. There is, however, one fragment of painting – a representation of SS. Constantine and Helena in the south porch, in an *al secco* technique rarely found in Russia at this period – which most scholars are inclined to date as early as the 11th century.

From the 12th century, when Novgorod became a republic ruled by the *Veche*, St Sophia was the principal church of the city. Dominating the town and the surrounding district, it seemed to symbolise the power and spiritual magnificence of Novgorod. Within the precincts of the church were established a magnificent library and a school. Here the local chroniclers began to record the history of their town, and within these walls were preserved splendid works of art and craftsmanship (including jewellery manufactured both in Novgorod and in other cities), the study of which might enable the local artists to perfect their skills. Finally St Sophia was used for the reception of foreign ambassadors and other visitors, and its galleries and vaults provided safe keeping for the city treasury.

In the first quarter of the 12th century a number of large churches were also built in the Commercial Quarter, and building continued on the left bank of the Volkhov. The most original building belonging to this period is the Cathedral of St George (1119), in the princely Yuryev Monastery (the Monastery of St George). Its stair-tower is built as a direct continuation of the west front, forming a rectangular projection only on the north side. The result was to produce an unusual arrangement of the domes: if these are joined by imaginary straight lines they form a triangle whose vertex lies slightly to one side, above the tower.

We can gather that the citizens of Novgorod were proud of this church, for the local chronicler, who is very sparing of references to individuals, records in his account of the building of the Cathedral of St George that "Master Peter laboured on this work".

In the thirties of the 12th century a rising which had long been brewing came to a head at last, and many were the citizens who lost their lives in street clashes or were thrown from the Volkhov bridge into the river. The princedom of Novgorod was transformed into a republic of boyars and merchants ruled by a popular assembly. The *kreml* now became the residence of the Archbishop and the Mayor, the leading personalities of the city, while the Princes moved to the old fortress of Rurik, where a *terem* (tower, keep) had been built in 1103.

The last princely church to be built in Novgorod was the Church of the Saviour on the Nereditsa (1198). This is a very different type of building from the grandiose cathedrals of the 11th and 12th centuries. It is a small whitewashed church with a single dome, a plain façade divided into three parts, and three apses, the two lateral apses being much lower than the central one. All the lines of the building are uneven and irregular, almost as if moulded freehand. For a building of such small size the walls are unnecessarily thick. In the west front is an entrance leading up to the gallery, supported not on vaulting but on wooden joists, which opens into the space under the dome only on the west side.

The interior of the church was decorated with paintings, on the usual subjects – illustrations of the Gospels and figures of prophets, celestial warriors and men of God. These sturdy broad-shouldered figures with rugged, austere faces, directing a piercing stare on the worshippers below or contemplating them mournfully from under lowered eyelids, seemed to be urging them to repentance with every fibre of their body and reminding them of the approach of the great Judgment Day – of which there was a grandiose representation on the west wall of the church.

The great company represented on the walls was not, however, confined exclusively to men of the Church. In the centre of the west wall was a portrait of the founder of the Nereditsa Church, Prince Yaroslav, offering a model of his church to Christ enthroned *(Plate p. 53)*.

Until the second world war the Nereditsa was almost the only mediaeval church in the whole of Europe which still preserved its painted decoration intact. Its destruction is an irreparable loss both to art historians and to lovers of art. When the German army was attacking Novgorod its artillery bombarded the Nereditsa at point-blank range, and the church was completely ruined. After the war it was rebuilt; but there could be no question of restoring the 12th century paintings which had been reduced to dust and ashes.

The modest architecture of the Nereditsa Church indicates that the Prince's treasury was now in low water; and it also points to another, much more important, fact—the increasing democratisation of taste. The boyars and merchants now frequently joined with the inhabitants of a particular street or district to carry out building work; and this widening of the architects' clientèle inevitably led to compromises in design. The churches were now smaller, almost square in plan, with a single dome supported on four piers. The stair-towers disappeared, and the open galleries gave place to closed chambers, in one of which was a kind of private chapel dedicated to the donor's patron saint. The Nereditsa is a typical example of this style of church.

Many churches were built by craft corporations or "brotherhoods" and by merchants' guilds. The chroniclers could barely keep pace with the new building: foundations of new churches might have to be recorded several times a year. Some of the merchants' churches were used as a place for keeping their business accounts, or standard weights and measures, or their most precious wares; for the stout stone walls of the churches provided greater security than the timber-walled store-rooms in their houses. And it was natural that when the structure of the church was put to such practical uses no one should be concerned about the beauty of the architecture or the decoration of the walls: the church had merely to provide accommodation for the faithful of the parish and to be stoutly and strongly built.

Then came the 13th century and the Mongol invasion. As we have seen, Novgorod escaped the worst of the devastation wrought by the Tatars in Russia; but it was, nevertheless, indirectly affected by the invasion. Moreover it had troubles of its own—the struggle with the Swedes and the knights of the Teutonic Order, which ended only with the victories of Alexander Nevsky (the Battle of the Neva in 1240 and the "Battle on the Ice" on Lake Peipus in 1243). Accordingly between the thirties and forties of the 13th century and the beginning of the 14th the artistic life of Novgorod was at a low ebb. This is particularly evident in architecture, for in the prevailing atmosphere of gloom and uncertainty about the future people had neither the resources nor the desire to build on the same scale as in earlier times. The main building effort was concentrated on fortifications, and the only churches recorded by the chroniclers as having been erected between 1240 and 1290 are three modest wooden structures.

In the 14th century, however, Lord Novgorod the Great enjoyed a fresh period of prosperity. Convoys of merchant ships again sailed the seas, and as in earlier times Novgorod despatched naval escorts to meet foreign traders and accompany them from Lake Ladoga up the River Volkhov to the city. From this period until the middle of the 15th century Novgorod once again became one of the most powerful and most prosperous of Russian cities.

In art the first signs of this revival can be seen in the closing years of the 13th century, with the building of the Church of St Nicholas-in-Lipna at the mouth of the River Msta on Lake Ilmen. (The name comes from the old Slavonic word *lipna*, a swamp or bog: the church was surrounded by swamp land). Some of its architectural features—the roof borne on a trefoil arch with a much heightened middle section, the absence of subdivisions in the external walls, the single squat apse, the single dome— represent the beginning of a new period in the history of the architecture of Novgorod.

The Church of the Dormition at Volotovo,[1] built in 1352 (and destroyed during the second world war), reproduced the same type with only minor changes ; and this trend was further developed in the Church of St Theodore Stratilates (1361) and the Church of the Transfiguration in the Commercial Quarter (1374).

Apart from the fact that St Theodore's roof is borne on a trefoil arch, while the Transfiguration has a hipped roof with four gables, both churches are remarkably similar. Both of them have a single dome, a single apse and a tripartite division of the external walls, and both—rather unexpectedly for Novgorod—are of considerable elegance. The apses are decorated with slender colonnettes linked by arches; under the domes are bands of dentils and triangular indentations; above the windows are semicircular ribs like eyebrows; and scattered about the walls, with no regard for symmetry, are a variety of rosettes and crosses, either carved in relief or hollowed out of the wall, and niches of varying shapes and sizes. The decoration undoubtedly shows the influence of ornament carved from wood.

Both churches were so much to the taste of the citizens of Novgorod that many contemporary and later buildings either imitated them or were mere variations of the same type. But with the exception of the Church of SS. Peter and Paul at Kozhevniki (1406) all these churches fall short of their models: one seems too wide for its height, in another the dome appears unduly massive, and so on.

We learn from the chronicler that the Church of the Transfiguration was decorated with paintings by Theophanes the Greek (Feofan Grek). Before coming to Russia Theophanes, a Byzantine by origin, had worked in Constantinople, Galata, Chalcedon and Caffa (Feodosiya in the Crimea), where he was said to have decorated more than forty churches. In Russia he worked in Novgorod and, at the beginning of the 15th century, in Moscow. The only wall paintings which can be ascribed to him with complete confidence, however, are the frescoes in the Church of the Transfiguration.

Theophanes was a bold and spirited artist; and it was remarked by contemporaries that he never painted from models, as was the accepted practice of the day, but relied entirely on his soaring imagination. Whether he was painting youthful angels or grey-haired hermits, his figures were filled with an intense inner life: sometimes sorrowing, sometimes absorbed in contemplation, they speak directly to us in the wordless language of painting.

Theophanes has a very individual style, highly generalised, almost impressionistic. He was fond of warm tones of yellow and brownish-orange (in faces, hands, clothing, or haloes) against a contrasting

---

[1] The name Volotovo is thought to be derived from the name of the pagan Slav god Veles or Volos (cf. p. 83), whose shrine seems to have stood on this spot in earlier days. The practice of building churches on the sites of former pagan temples was commonly found in the early Middle Ages not only in Russia but in western Europe.

ground painted in shades of cold greyish-blue, greyish-green or greyish-violet. He rendered masses not only by the use of deep shadows but also by bold lines of white emphasising the areas of greatest relief.

One of the most impressive pieces of painting in the Church of the Transfiguration is the figure of St Macarius the Egyptian *(Plate p. 56)*. He is represented as a majestic old man with his hands raised in the gesture of prayer. His swarthy face stands out against the mass of white hair which falls to his shoulders and merges with his long grey beard. Under his sorrowfully knitted brows, which cast a shadow over almost the whole of the upper part of his face, his eyes shine from behind half-lowered lids, giving a melancholy austerity to his glance. The pose in full face, the severely vertical lines of the figure and the exact correspondence between the positions of the two hands create an impression of immobility, of serene solemnity, which is in sharp contrast with the internal tension expressed in the face and the eyes. We feel the great force of this inspired figure, which owes its effect mainly to Theophanes' free and impressionistic manner. The bold strokes which delineate the hair, the beard and the clothing of this saintly hermit seem to have been drawn by the hand of a giant.

An artist of powerful and individual talent and at the same time a man of wide culture, Theophanes made a great impression on his contemporaries. All who came into contact with this gifted painter were hard put to it to decide which was the more remarkable—his dexterity with the brush, his powerful imagination, his vigorous personality or the good sense of his discourse.

In any account of the art of mediaeval Novgorod icon-painting must occupy a special place. We possess considerable numbers of icons from this period; and indeed, as we have already noted, it is mainly from them that we draw our knowledge of the development of Russian painting in the 13th and 14th centuries. The word icon is derived from the Greek *eikon*, an image or representation. Icons were painted on wooden panels, which in the case of larger works might be built up from a number of separate boards joined by wooden pins and dowels. On the front of the panel a rectangular cavity known as the "ark" or "shrine" was hollowed out, leaving a slightly raised rim which served as a kind of frame. Then the panel was covered, either in whole or in part, with canvas, and on top of this was applied a ground coat made from a mixture of powdered alabaster or chalk and animal glue. On this the painting was done in tempera (i.e., with colours based on an egg-yolk medium). The colours were used either in the pure state or mixed to produce various shades; much use was also made of gilding.

It is scarcely necessary to enumerate the range of subjects depicted in icons, for these are fairly generally known: we shall merely note, as occasion arises, certain subjects which fall outside the usual repertoire. At the outset, however, one significant point must be referred to—the fact that the icons representing saints almost outnumber all the others put together. The reason for this is clear. To the people of the period with which we are concerned the saints were intermediaries between them and God, ever ready to intervene on their behalf and to intercede for them. Invisible, usually benevolent but occasionally terrible in their wrath, the saints were always at a man's side, taking the liveliest interest in all his worldly concerns throughout his life from the cradle to the grave.

When a child was born, therefore, its parents hastened to have it baptised within a week—for one never knows what mishap may befall a child and the Devil is always lying in wait for an unchristened soul. The child was given the name of a saint, usually the saint on whose day the christening took place, and thereafter it had its own guardian angel, ready until its dying day to preserve it from all ills.

Then as time went on childhood passed into adolescence, and soon it was necessary to decide what business or trade a youth should follow. But when a man of the Middle Ages chose a particular occupation he acquired another patron saint—sometimes, indeed, two. If he decided to become a blacksmith or a doctor he came under the protection of SS. Cosmas and Damian; the patron of carpenters and boatwrights was St Nicholas, of well-diggers St Theodore Tiro or St Theodore Stratilates. The protector of gardeners was St Spiridion, of stock-rearers St Blaise (Vlasy), the ancient Slav "cattle god" Veles now transformed into a Christian saint and retaining the same functions as in his pagan incarnation. The particular duties assigned to certain saints were remarkably varied. St George the Victorious, for example, was the guardian of ploughmen and shepherds; but he was also the patron of all Russian warriors, so that his cult achieved particular popularity during the struggle with the Mongols. In a word, all forms of human activity were at this period under the protection of the saints. Even the horse-coper had his own particular patron, St Parasceve or St Pyatnitsa ("St Friday"). St Parasceve—together with St Anastasia, with whom she was often represented—was also responsible for trade and commerce, and accordingly churches dedicated to her were built in the market-places of the mediaeval Russian cities; and, by the same token, fairs were held on Fridays. St Parasceve also had certain duties more appropriate to her sex, for she was regarded as the patron saint of women's domestic tasks. And woe betide any over-industrious housewife who sat up until midnight on Friday at her spinning instead of paying honour to her patroness on her own particular day! For then St Parasceve would cause sleep to overcome her unfaithful servant and would plague her by throwing ashes and flax-combings into her eyes.

When anything went wrong in a man's household or business he appealed at once for the help of the saints. If a thief broke in by night St Theodore Tiro was applied to for the return of the stolen property. If the hens were laying badly St Mamas would be asked for help; if the cow fell sick it was a matter for St Blaise. The mediaeval saints thus took on their shoulders all the worries and anxieties of the ordinary people who looked to them for assistance and protection.

The folk calendar, and with it the regular round of work in the household and in the fields, was built up round a succession of saints' days, and this is reflected in a whole series of proverbs and popular saws. "St Dmitry needs no ferryman", was one old saying: this meant that from the 26th October, St Dmitry's name-day, the rivers could be expected to freeze. On St George's Day, 23rd April, the cattle were driven out to pasture for the first time after the winter: hence the saying, "St George comes in with the grass". The careless peasant who had not laid in a store of hay in good time knew that his last chance was on St Procopius' Day, 8th July, the latest possible day for haymaking. In consequence the unfortunate saint acquired the rather disparaging nickname of St Procopius Lazy-Scythe. We find the same kind of thing in the kitchen and backyard. "Cut your cabbages—don't wait for the Protection" (the feast of the Protection of the Virgin, 1st October) was the admonition addressed by zealous housewives to their younger and less conscientious sisters. And an abundance of similar examples could be quoted from all the varied activities of human life.

It is easy, therefore, to see why icons were of such importance to the people of this period. They were not found only in churches, but were an essential element in the furnishing of every dwelling house, from a prince's mansion to the meanest peasant's hut. The number and artistic quality of the

icons in a man's house were taken as an indication of his degree of prosperity in the same way as, for example, the number of gold and silver vessels displayed on his sideboard.

The icons were hung in rows in a special corner of the living room. Each one was covered with a screen to protect it from the dust, and the whole corner was draped with a curtain of heavy, solid material. In a wealthy household the edges and background of an icon were covered with an *oklad* (frame) of gold or silver, embossed or chased. Below the icons were splendid hangings, usually of satin, embroidered with silk and metal brocade and pearls. The corner with the icons was a central feature of the house, as is indicated by its popular name of *krasny kut*, the "fair corner".

The houses of the wealthy contained a special room known as the "room of the Cross", one wall of which was completely covered with icons. When the owner of the house had a domestic chaplain divine service was celebrated in this room.

Icons were also hung at the entrances of houses in order to ensure divine protection for the occupants; on the gates of stables in order that SS. Florus and Laurus, the saintly horse-breeders, might drive away the mischievous imps who tied elf-knots in the horses' manes; on wells, so that St Theodore Tiro (or his twin, St Theodore Stratilates), spear at the ready, might keep a watchful eye on the water-sprite, lest he should carry off some thoughtless woman come to draw water. At crossroads, special posts were erected on which icons were mounted under a protective roof; for it was well known that the Evil One was accustomed to lurk about such places under cover of night.

In the popular mind the saint and his representation on an icon were inseparably linked: the icon was a kind of materialised image of the saint. If a worshipper's prayers were answered he would express his gratitude to the icon in suitable fashion: a man of small means might offer a candle costing three *altyns*, a more prosperous citizen might present a string of coloured beads or an embroidered pall, or perhaps a costly *oklad* for the icon. But if a prayer went unheard the icon might be "punished" by the removal of its *oklad* and decorative hangings, or even by having its face turned to the wall.

This matter-of-fact and businesslike attitude led to a very considerable demand for icons. In the 16th and 17th centuries, and perhaps even earlier, there were special stalls for icons in the market-places, at which a purchaser might acquire any particular icon which took his fancy. To talk of buying and selling, however, was regarded as unseemly; for a man who "bought" an icon would have been regarded as buying the saint himself. The convention, therefore, was to say that the icon had been "exchanged for money". If the seller thought that the customer was not offering enough he would push the money away without saying a word; and the process would continue until the two parties finally reached agreement on a price.

The owners of icons of high artistic quality treated them as cherished possessions, making special mention of them in their wills along with objects made of the precious metals. They were presented to the Tsar on the name-day of his patron saint, on the birth of an heir to the throne, and on other special occasions; and they were also offered to highly-placed officials and other important personages as a mark of high respect.

Icons do not as a rule make an immediate appeal to the modern eye on account of the distinctive features of their representational language, in which everything turns on a special system of symbolism.

This was to be expected in a period when the most ordinary phenomena of life were construed as good or bad omens, when the whole visible universe and the whole history of mankind were interpreted as a gigantic pattern of symbols. In mediaeval painting almost every figure, in addition to its immediate representational significance, also had another meaning–Christ or the Virgin, The Christian Church or one of the sacraments, or some particular idea or event. Thus the three Kings in the Nativity personified the three ages of man–youth, maturity and old age– and were depicted accordingly in the icons. And again there was a symbolic idea behind this personification : all mankind, young and old, were called on to worship Christ. The gifts brought by the three Kings were also symbolical : they offered the Child "gold, as to a king; frankincense, as to God; and myrrh, as to a dead man". Many other scenes represented in icons were also of symbolic significance : the Fall and the Expulsion from Paradise, for example, represented the redeeming sacrifice of Christ. Even the placing of the figures had its own symbolism : thus in the Last Judgment the foolish virgins symbolised the rejected sinners and stood on Christ's left, while the wise virgins represented the blessed and were placed on His right hand. Finally there was a whole symbolism of gesture : a hand pressed against the cheek indicated grief, while a hand held out with open palm was a sign of submission. There were also a great variety of attributes associated with particular figures. Angels would often have pilgrims' staffs in their hands, indicating their rôle as divine messengers; martyrs had crosses, as a sign that they had suffered for the Faith; bishops carried the Gospels; prophets had scrolls of documents; and the magnanimous and benevolent SS. Cosmas and Damian could be recognised as doctors from the boxes of medicine they carried. It would be easy to multiply the examples.

Symbolism, indeed, runs through the whole of mediaeval painting. In many Novgorod icons of the 13th and 14th centuries one of the figures is represented on a much larger scale than the others– sometimes because he is the leading figure in the scene (in the case of St John, St George and St Blaise, for example) *(Plate p. 55)*, sometimes because he also personifies the victory of the forces of light over the forces of darkness (e.g., St George in the icons representing "St George and the Dragon") *(Plate p. 64)*. And again many other examples could be quoted.

This symbolism of ideas leads to a symbolism of artistic expression. When the icon-painter requires to indicate a particular locality he employs a whole system of distinguishing marks, using the part to represent the whole. A blue segment sprinkled with gold dots in the upper part of a picture represents the firmament with its spangle of stars. Two trees—sometimes only one—serve to represent a forest or, in some cases, the Earthly Paradise; a small tower stands for a palace, a battlemented wall for a town. If a character is seated on a stool, or is associated with a table or some other item of domestic furnishing, this indicates that the action is taking place indoors. Sometimes, to put the matter beyond doubt, the artist paints a little tower or house, covered with drapery, *(velum)*, on either side of the central figure.

One of the principal conventions of mediaeval painting is the method of representing the succession of events in time. The method of representation is of necessity conventional, for the expression of the passage of time lies quite outside the proper scope of painting. The painter is concerned not with temporal but with spatial relationships: he can show the development of an action in space but not in time. The mediaeval icon-painter, bringing together into a single moment of time a series of events which took place over a period, crowding into a restricted space the whole wide expanse of the world, combines in a single composition a variety of episodes from a particular story, showing what took place before the principal event and what came after it. Moreover in representing the characters involved in these various episodes he may sometimes disregard the proper sequence of events, mingling earlier occurrences with later or showing the same characters several times. Thus in icons of the Nativity we see a whole series of events represented simultaneously—the Nativity itself, the angels telling the good tidings to the shepherds, the three Kings travelling from the East, Joseph in the desert talking to a herdsman, and, finally, midwives preparing to bathe the Child. (There is a magnificent 15th century icon from Novgorod on this subject in the Tretyakov Gallery). Nor did anyone take it amiss if an icon showed Jerusalem situated close to Constantinople, or even to Moscow; for the mediaeval Russian icon-painter (and for that matter his contemporaries in western Europe) had no conception of time or of distance.

Another important characteristic is that the icon-painters—and indeed mediaeval painters in general—strove to represent their subjects in a single plane. They achieved this in a variety of ways, but principally by the use of inverse perspective. The technique is based on a genuine reversed perspective and is not merely a distorted version of regular linear perspective. In using it the artist was governed by a set of definite rules: the difference was that the vanishing point was not in the background of the picture but out in front, as if it were in the eye of the person looking at the picture. In consequence the objects represented did not appear smaller as they receded into the background—as they do in modern painting and in the real world—but grew larger. In other words, in icon-painting volumes and distances are, as it were, turned inside out. The effect of a single plane is obtained also by making figures in the foreground and the background of the same size: indeed the more distant figures are sometimes larger than the nearer.

Finally we come to what is perhaps the most important element in painting—the use of colour. The icon-painter used flat primary colours, with no variation of tone over the painted area. Such colours always produce the impression of a plane surface, particularly where they show no variation in luminosity—that is, where the artist does not use darker or lighter tones. The combination of large surfaces evenly covered with flat colours is one of the principal means of achieving a uniform pattern in a single plane—an effect based on the arrangement of all the figures and objects represented in the picture. For the icon-painter this technique is a source of unity and harmony, and consequently of beauty. The reader must not, however, suppose that this flatness of the decorative surface is a purely formal effect. On the contrary, it contributes to the revelation of the content; for the concordance of forms and colours, combined with the rhythmic unity, is one of the most effective means of linking the different figures in a composition.

These features of the icon-painters' technique are a reflection of mediaeval patterns of thought, with their abstractness, their symbolism, and their desire to ensure that the sacred events represented in these paintings were set apart from the regular round of everyday life. It was a very understandable desire, for the heroes represented by the mediaeval painter were very unlike ordinary people. They lived in a world of signs and wonders, and could themselves work wonders: they were indifferent to the joys of earthly life; they could read the thoughts in men's minds, they understood the language of animals and birds, and the secrets of the future were known to them. An ordinary mortal could not but feel the infinite distance which separated him from the saint looking down on him from an icon. For if the saint had been no different from an ordinary man, where would his special virtue have lain, and how could he have been of any help to men in the trials and sorrows of their life on earth? Hence the artistic canons laid down by the Church for the icon-painter, the obligatory system of iconography, the practice of painting from models or from "painters' guides" *(podlinniki)*. The model was often provided by some particularly famous icon, but there were also special iconographical handbooks or guides.

Of particular interest are the "illustrated guides". These are arranged according to the regular sequence of the months in the year, beginning with September (the first month in the ancient Russian year), the days of the month and the days of the week. On each page the various festivals and saints are shown under the appropriate dates. The figures are represented in outline, with some indication also of the internal outlines—the features, the details and the folds of the clothing, with a light monotone shading to render the volumes. Short notes on each picture draw attention to particular characteristics of the type or to the colours used in the clothing. The icon-painter had a guide of this kind in front of him as he worked. To paint without a model was something quite out of the ordinary: we remember, for example, how a contemporary, discussing the artistic technique of Theophanes the Greek, remarked particularly on the fact that he did not follow any model.

Thus, from whatever aspect we consider it, Russian icon-painting was a highly conventional art. We must not forget, however, that the artist was a sentient human being who was not blind to the world which surrounded him; and wherever it was possible without prejudice to the central conception of his work and his personal artistic vision, and without departing from the strict requirements of ecclesiastical doctrine, he incorporated in his painting some particle of the real world, some feature observed in his everyday experience. He did this right up to the end of the 16th century—admittedly on a very small scale, perhaps even unconsciously; but he did it none the less, as the reader can readily see from the illustrations.

In discussing the work of the icon-painters of Novgorod we need say little about the icons of the 12th century, which—like those produced in other parts of Russia at this period—are to a greater or lesser extent under Byzantine influence. With rare exceptions they all show the same swarthy faces of Oriental cast with large dark eyes, either severe or sorrowful, the same rather sombre colouring in which various shades of ochre predominate. It is characteristic of the 12th century icons that they show only one or two figures against a plain background. Fixed in their rigid poses for all eternity, indifferent to one another and to the whole surrounding world, these figures seem to be suspended in a vacuum, an empty space painted in gold or silver, or sometimes coloured. This is the standard style of the period, and there are very few departures from it.

In the 13th century, however—at an earlier period than in other Russian towns—there grew up in Novgorod a local school of icon-painting with its own distinctive characteristics. As we have noted, Novgorod did not suffer from the Mongol invasion to the same extent as other parts of Russia; and icon-painting in particular continued to develop there throughout these years of tribulation. Indeed—paradoxical though it may seem at first sight—the Mongol invasion itself promoted the rapid development of a local school in Novgorod, since it led to the interruption of the long-standing links between Novgorod and Byzantium. As a result the local painters, freed from the artistic dominance of Constantinople, were compelled to rely only on their own personal judgments and standards, and to adapt their style to local preferences: and as time went on these local trends became still more firmly established. During the 13th century the faces of the saints in the icons begin to take on definite Russian characteristics, and sometimes even exhibit a distinctive Novgorod type. The smooth Byzantine manner gives place to a more vigorous style—one which is sometimes rather crude but is always expressive. Sharp colour contrasts are sometimes met with—for example red and greenish-blue. A ground colour of bright cinnabar red now came into use, and became so popular that it is found right into the 15th century.

The great period of Novgorod icon-painting was in the 14th and 15th centuries. Bright, joyous colours replace the restrained, austere hues of the earlier period. The figures of saints in individual icons increase in number and are reduced in size. Representations of particular scenes become increasingly popular; and it is noteworthy that the vigorous activity of the men of Novgorod is reflected in a similar vigour in their saints. In the icons belonging to these centuries the figures are represented in motion, in a range of different—though not very varied—activities and attitudes. Each of these figures is engaged in some particular action: Abraham and Sarah busy themselves with the entertainment of the three angels *(Plate p. 66)*, St George rides full tilt at the dragon *(Plate p. 64)*, St Nikita (Nicetas) thrashes a demon with a cudgel, Jesus leads Adam and Eve out of the fiery furnace, and so on. The plain monotone backgrounds have disappeared, at least in representations of particular scenes. The citizens of Novgorod in this period were not fond of the diffuse and indefinite, and the icon-painter sought, while preserving the characteristics we have already discussed, to indicate the setting of the action ; and accordingly buildings, trees and rocky caverns now begin to appear in the background of the icons. Backgrounds consisting of a plain paint wash are found only in icons forming part of a set or tier *(chin)* on an iconostasis, for example a *deesis* or a company of prophets. As instances we may take the icons of the Archangel Michael or St Barbara *(Plate p. 61)*, who provided protection against fire or the perils of the sea (both in the Tretyakov Gallery). We may note incidentally that the Novgorod icons of the 14th century frequently show a combination of different techniques, using graphic methods in drawing the clothing and paint in the treatment of faces—a feature found, for example, in the works just mentioned.

Of special interest, however, are the icons representing particular scenes. It is in these that we find the artist bringing in details from everyday life. We may take as an example a scene from the margin of an icon devoted to the life of St George, an early work belonging to the beginning of the 14th century *(Plate p. 68)*. This represents one of the martyrdoms suffered by the saint, showing him immersed to the waist in a cauldron of boiling oil, with his hands raised in the gesture of prayer and his eyes turned up to heaven, preaching to a congregation of listeners who are outside the picture. The sermon he is preaching must be an eloquent one, for it has touched even the hardened hearts of the two tormentors who are engaged in stoking the fire under the cauldron ; one of them is holding one hand to his ear, as if afraid of missing a single word, while the other is wiping away tears of emotion. And there are a wealth of similar lively touches in an icon of the Nativity of the Virgin *(Plate p. 62)* dating from the late 14th or the 15th century (now, like the St George already mentioned, in the Russian Museum in Leningrad), and in many other Novgorod icons of the same period on the same theme: a maid is carefully smoothing the mother's pillow, a nurse is bending over the cradle as if singing a lullaby, another is keeping flies away from the sleeping child with a fan; or again we see two wooden poles arched over the cradle as a support for muslin curtains—a type of cradle which is still occasionally seen today. Another curious detail may be quoted to show that icons, as well as delighting the eye of the art lover, also provide valuable information for the historian and student of manners. In the icon we have been discussing, the women who come to visit the mother are carrying gold and silver vessels; and in some representations of the Nativity of the Virgin these vessels are shown without lids and are seen to contain coins. From time immemorial it had been the custom to present a newly born infant with cups or goblets of precious metal filled with gold and silver coins. The literary sources refer to this custom in the 17th century; and the icons provide proof that the practice was known in Russia at a much earlier period—at least as early as the 14th century.

One 15th century Novgorod icon of special interest is the "Battle of the Men of Suzdal with the Men of Novgorod", formerly known as the "Miracle of the Icon of the Sign" (Plate p. 63). The picture is based on a real event—the siege of Novgorod in 1169-1170 by the army of Prince Andrey Bogolyubsky of Vladimir-Suzdal; and the icon, which is divided into three registers, illustrates the various episodes of the story in proper sequence.

The chronicler tells us that shortly before the siege an angel appeared to John, Archbishop of Novgorod, telling him that the men of Novgorod would be victorious if the icon of Our Lady of the Sign were placed on the walls of the citadel. (The icons of this iconographical type represent the Virgin with her hands raised in prayer; on her breast, usually in a round medallion, is a half-length figure of a young and beardless Christ, in the same posture as His Mother). The icon-painter begins his story at the moment when the icon is carried out of the church; and since the story is concerned with a real and local event the setting is precisely defined. In the uppermost register we see the two districts of Novgorod—the St Sophia Quarter, easily recognisable from the fortifications of the citadel and the domes of the cathedral, and the Commercial Quarter, identified by the Church of the Transfiguration. The two districts are joined by the bridge over the Volkhov, shown exactly as it is described in the chronicles—built of timber, with no hand-rail, and supported on timber piers. The Archbishop hands the icon over to a deacon, and we then see them crossing the bridge, with the boyars and the people coming out of the citadel to meet them. Thus, in order to show the development of the subject in time, following the principle we have already discussed, the Prince and his clergy are represented twice in the same composition. In the middle register the story reaches its climax. The icon now stands on one of the towers of the citadel; within the walls can be seen the warriors of Novgorod, and facing them are the forces of Suzdal; and on both sides is a forest of lances and triumphantly waving banners. Three horsemen ride out from the besieging army, and three others emerge from the gates of the city to meet them. It looks as if a parley is to be held; but this is not to be. Unable to control their impatience, the men of Suzdal loose their bow-strings and a hail of fiery arrows flies against the icon. Such blasphemy is not to be endured, and the warriors of Novgorod surge out from the citadel, led by four saintly champions—George the Victorious, SS. Boris and Gleb, and Alexander Nevsky. Their lances are pointed against the enemy, as is the naked sword borne by an angel who flies down from Heaven. The result of the battle is a foregone conclusion. The front ranks of the army of Suzdal stand their ground, and the bodies of the fallen are trampled under the hooves of the horses; but the rear ranks break and flee. This icon is the first intimation of an important stage in the development of Russian painting, the emergence of the new *genre* of the historical battle picture; for this icon is essentially a battle picture, painted according to the traditions of icon-painting merely because in the circumstances of the time there was no alternative.

The reason for the choice of such an unusual subject for an icon, and for its occurrence in Novgorod of all places (and the popularity of the theme in Novgorod in the second half of the 15th century is shown by the fact that we possess three variants of the same subject—in the Novgorod Museum, the Russian Museum in Leningrad and the Tretyakov Gallery) is of some interest. Basically the reason is a political one. Novgorod had long been resisting the centralising tendencies of Moscow, sometimes indeed going so far as to betray the wider interests of Russia: during the decisive moments of the struggle with the Mongols, for example, only Ryazan and Novgorod failed to send their forces to take part in the Battle of Kulikovo. In the 15th century, when the friction with Moscow was particularly acute, a number of literary works were produced in Novgorod celebrating the city's earlier glories and remembering the great deeds done in the past. In 1430, for example, there appeared a new literary account of the memorable battle with the men of Suzdal in the 12th century, which now included the "Tale of the Miracles of the Icon of the Sign" (unlike the earlier chronicle, which was simple and straightforward, with no miracles). This account tells how during the attack by the army of Suzdal the icon, having been hit by their arrows, shed tears and turned away from the enemy; and then "there fell darkness upon them... and blinded them, every man". The icon-painter shows us nothing of this miracle, but he does depict another—the appearance of the warrior saints, of whom there is no mention in the chronicle. The significance of this is clear: if Moscow seeks to interfere with the independence of Novgorod then she will find not only the people of Novgorod but all the hosts of Heaven ranged against her. Even the patron saint of Suzdal, Boris (who had been Prince of Rostov) was on the side of Novgorod, to say nothing of St George and Alexander Nevsky, the invincible champion of the men of Novgorod. The appearance of Alexander Nevsky on the icon is of course a complete anachronism, for he was born half a century after the siege of Novgorod by Andrey Bogolyubsky. But in the Middle Ages no one was concerned about such historical inconsistencies, particularly in works of an allegorical character.

The subject of the "Battle of the Men of Suzdal with the Men of Novgorod" and the circumstances which dictated this choice of subject make this work, of course, unique among 15th century icons. But certain features of this icon, in particular the painter's striving for a narrative effect, were to become distinctive characteristics of the painting of the following century. This interest in telling a story was so strong that we sometimes find the icon-painter introducing various details which are of purely anecdotal significance. As an example we may take the icon of the "Miracle of St George and the Dragon", *(Plate p. 65)* of the early 16th century (now in the Russian Museum). A huge figure of St George on horseback, wearing golden armour and a flowing scarlet cloak, fills almost the whole panel; in comparison with him the other figures represented in the icon seem pigmies. This is quite as it should be, for St George is the principal character in the icon, and moreover represents the victory of Heaven over the forces of Hell. This is indicated by the right hand of God which is seen in a gesture of blessing against a segment of blue sky and by the angel who is flying down to offer the victorious saint a golden crown. On the left is a tall tower, the open galleries of which are thronged with people, and under the arch of the lowerst storey is a princess holding the tamed dragon on a halter. Against the balcony on the first floor stands a ladder, and a young man is climbing up this ladder in great haste, taking two or three rungs at a time and looking over his shoulder quickly to see whether the monster is still pursuing him. The people on the balcony hasten to pull him over the balustrade. One of them, however, cowers back, trying to pull his cloak over his face; but his curiosity overcomes his fear and he remains fixed in his pose, his face half concealed by his cloak. In the gallery on the second storey are the Prince and Princess with their whole court; and on the summit of the tower are two heralds, proclaiming with their trumpets to all the surrounding district the happy outcome of the combat. The whole work radiates a mood of triumphant celebration, which is expressed chiefly in the treatment of the theme but is reinforced by the bright clear colours, in which scarlet and emerald green predominate.

These bright colours are perhaps the only feature which recalls the icon-painting of an earlier period. Elsewhere we see the imprint of the style of Moscow (e.g., in the elegance of line, the occasional triviality of form and almost miniature-like refinement of the painting, the striving for decorative effect both in the composition as a whole and in the detail). Later Novgorod icons of the 16th and 17th centuries are sometimes very difficult to distinguish from Muscovite work. The influence of Moscow was also felt in architecture. The whole of the art of Novgorod, in fact, lost its particular regional colouring during the last two centuries of the older Russia. What, we may wonder, had caused this change?

Even in the architecture of Novgorod in the 15th century we feel that the creative urge has lost something of its former vigour. In the boyars' churches, for example, we find no more than variations on the 14th century models which had achieved such popularity. Archbishop Euthymius II (1429-1458) devoted much effort to the building of monasteries outside the city walls and to the restoration of older buildings reconstructed in later periods, which he now sought to restore to their original appearance. Almost the only really new building of the period was the Archbishop's Mansion *(Vladychnaya Palata)* (1433), the first secular building in Russia designed specifically for a public purpose. Its well-preserved Hall of Justice is of strikingly unusual construction, with a square pier in the centre supporting the groined vaulting. This first—and last—appearance of Gothic in mediaeval Russia is explained by the fact that craftsmen from the Baltic towns were associated with the master builders of Novgorod in the construction of the Mansion.

This return to the architectural types and forms of earlier centuries flowed from the same causes as the choice of subject in the icon of the "Battle of the Men of Suzdal with the Men of Novgorod": the frictions with Moscow which developed finally into open war. Matters reached such a pitch that the authorities of Novgorod put their territory under the protection of Lithuania. The moving spirit of the plot was the ambitious wife of the mayor of Novgorod, Boretsky, who is remembered in Russian history and literature as Marfa-Posadnitsa, Martha the Mayoress. The ordinary people, however, were unwilling to accept foreign overlordship. During the last siege of Novgorod by the Muscovite army in 1477 the gunners spiked the cannon on the ramparts of the city, and the townsfolk threw open the gates and swore allegiance to the Grand Prince. Sitting in the vaulted chamber of the Vladychnaya

Palata, Ivan III pronounced his decree: "No assembly bell shall there be in Novgorod, no mayor shall there be; our rule shall prevail."

The people of Novgorod remained largely indifferent to the fate of Martha the Mayoress and the other conspirators; but they were much distressed by the carrying off of their Assembly Bell to Moscow. For centuries its peals had sounded over Novgorod, many a time summoning the townsfolk to rise in rebellion. The people of Novgorod revered it as a symbol which enshrined their memories of the freedom they had enjoyed in the past and their dreams of future liberation.

A poetic old legend tells the story that when the bell was being transported through the Valday Hills in a sleigh—a scene represented in a miniature of the period—it refused to leave its native soil, jumped off the sleigh and broke into a thousand little bells, the "Valday bells" which used to tinkle in horses' harness, combining with the doleful singing of the coachmen to form a music which has been heard into our own day, carrying down through the centuries the memory of Lord Novgorod the Great.

Having discussed the art of Novgorod, we must now—in spite of the limitations on our space— say something about the art of Pskov. And indeed Pskov deserves a good deal more than a mere passing mention; for the history of the city contains many notable names and many notable events. There is, for example, the beautiful Princess Olga, wife of Igor son of Rurik, Prince of Kiev, who fell in battle against the Drevlyanians, and grandmother of Vladimir "Bright Sun", whom the chronicler calls the wisest of women; and there is Alexander Nevsky, the victor in the famous Battle on the Ice. Many stories and legends are associated with this area, which in the Middle Ages lay on the western boundary of the territory of Novgorod.

Lake Peipus, on which the Battle on the Ice was fought, is joined to the Lake of Pskov by a narrow ribbon of water, and at the south end of this lake, where the River Velikaya is joined by its tributary the Pskova just before it falls into the lake, the city of Pskov was established as early as the 11th century on a high rocky promontory within its protecting ramparts (which exist to this day, though mainly in the form of a 15th century reconstruction). They are traditionally associated with the name of the fair Princess Olga; but in fact "on whose authority and by what people the city was established" even the chroniclers cannot tell.

During the early part of its history Pskov was a dependency of Novgorod, ruled by the Princes of Novgorod and their henchmen and subject in all important matters to the *Veche* of Novgorod. The city took part, however, in Novgorod's trade with the East and the West and rapidly grew rich. Then the wars with the Swedes and the knights of the Livonian Order, in which Novgorod many times left Pskov to its fate, taught the people of Pskov the love of freedom and the consciousness of their own strength. At any rate by the middle of the 14th century Pskov had become the "younger brother of Novgorod the Great", the second feudal republic in the history of mediaeval Russia.

The works of art produced in Pskov in the 12th and 13th centuries bear witness to the city's close connections with other parts of Russia, in particular Polotsk and Smolensk, and also with Byzantium. The cathedral in the Ivanovsky Monastery, built in the first half of the 13th century, shows clearly that its architect was inspired by the work of the master builder of Novgorod, Master Peter. Even in this early period, however, the general trend of the local architecture is entirely individual and is determined by the particular circumstances of the area. Thus perhaps nowhere else in Russia were such large numbers of fortifications erected as in the Pskov area, for this was a form of building made necessary by the constant wars fought over this territory. These local fortresses were known for the quality of their building : the Germans gave Izborsk, for example, the name of Eisenburg, the "iron stronghold".

The year 1348 marks the beginning of Pskov's political independence, which was to last for rather more than a hundred and fifty years. This was also the period of flowering of its art, which had now completely thrown off the influence of Novgorod. In Pskov everything was plainer and simpler than in its "elder brother", both in worldly matters and in the sphere of spiritual life. In general the Princes were of less importance in the life of Pskov, the boyars were not so rich and influential as in Novgorod, and in consequence the *Veche* had more power and the forms of government were more democratic. All this left its mark on the art of Pskov, and in particular on its architecture. Apart from the grandiose Cathedral of the Trinity (of which we have only a late 17th century reconstruction) the churches of Pskov are much simpler than those of Novgorod. They are small buildings with massive walls, usually with a single dome and a hipped roof, and with rectangular windows like ordinary houses. Their whole appearance, in fact, has something of the homeliness of a dwelling house. The rather cramped interiors of these churches are equally unassuming: usually they have no painting but are merely whitewashed. The lack of space within the churches themselves made it necessary to build on various chapels, covered porches and store-rooms; sometimes, indeed, the whole of the basement was given up to storage and similar purposes. This need cause no surprise, for the builders of the Pskov churches were for the most part the ordinary citizens of the town: churches built by boyars are of rare occurrence here. Frequently a belfry is built on to one of the annexes, or to the church itself, consisting of two or three piers supporting a crossbeam, sometimes with a pitched roof, with the bells hanging between the piers. It is these belfries which give the churches of Pskov their particular character. In this area, too, the churches were built in a matter-of-fact and easygoing way found nowhere else. The builders first built their church, and then considered to whom it should be dedicated: indeed the saint who should thus be honoured might be decided by the drawing of lots. The very names of the churches, too, strike us as familiar, almost lighthearted: the Church of St Basil the Great on the Hillock *(Plate p. 90)*, St Sergius Beyond the Ponds, St Nicholas in the Marsh, the Resurrection in the Pasture, and so on. It is significant also that there was relatively little monastery building in the territory of Pskov; and in general the monastic ideal had less influence in the sober and businesslike atmosphere that prevailed in Pskov than in other parts of mediaeval Russia.

Unlike Novgorod with its timber building, Pskov built most of its houses in stone. The material, in the form of the local flagstone, was readily at hand. The only buildings to have survived are a few 17th century merchants' houses, in particular the Pogankin House (now housing the local museum), a large two-storied building on a π-shaped plan in a severe, almost fortress-like, style of architecture. Evidently the 17th century, concerned as it was to dress up everything in the latest style, did not presume to interfere with Pskov, a city of warriors and of busy people who had no time for trifles.

Until quite recently the monumental art of Pskov was one of the least understood chapters in the history of mediaeval Russian art. The work of Soviet restorers and scholars, however, has thrown much light in these dark places. The frescoes in the cathedral of the Spaso-Mirozhsky Monastery (1156) were cleaned in 1926, and the paintings in the Church of the Nativity in the Snetogorsky Monastery in 1928-29, continuing in 1948-49. Some of the latter paintings show a strikingly original iconographic treatment, and one of the several different styles which have been identified here is curiously reminiscent of the work of a painter of a considerably later period, Theophanes the Greek. The paintings in the Church of the Nativity were apparently done soon after the building of the church, about the year 1313.

A beginning has also recently been made with the cleaning of the Pskov icons *(Plate p. 91)*, of which so far relatively few are known. In representations of particular scenes these commonly show figures in violent movement, in contrast with others which are quite motionless. The faces of the saints have a surprisingly terrestrial, almost coarse, quality. The colours most frequently used are black, red, white, dark yellow and green. It looks as if the painters of Pskov were faithful to the same ideals as the architects, preferring a style which is expressive but simple, reticent, and always closer to earth than to Heaven.

In 1510 the independence of the free city of Pskov came to an end, when with all its territories it became part of the princedom of Muscovy. The citizens of Pskov watched griefstruck as the Assembly Bell was taken down from the belfry of the Trinity Church in the citadel. Surprisingly, however, Pskov —unlike Novgorod—did not lose the distinctive features of its art when it was swallowed up in Muscovy. The churches of the 16th century can easily be taken for works of an earlier period, and the belfries of Pskov continued to be a distinctive feature of the urban scene into the 17th century.

Pskov's situation as a frontier town meant that the building of fortifications continued during the Muscovite period (or, as it would be more accurate to say, the period of a unified Russian state). In 1519 and 1524 the line of the outer city wall was continued beyond the River Pskova, and the famous Thundering Tower was built; then in the 1550s the defensive ramparts of the Pechorsky Monastery were constructed. Meanwhile, however, life flowed on in the ordinary way; within the city walls there was still the same bustle of activity in the market-place, and the craftsmen still sang as they bent over their work, just as they had done in earlier days.

Page from the Stroganov "Painters' Guide". 16th-17th centuries. (Ph. Novosti).

V Moscow, the Third Rome

In the first millennium A.D., as we know from archaeological excavation, there was a large Slav settlement on the banks of the River Moskva and the Yauza. Probably in the Middle Ages men laying the foundations of houses or digging into the earth for one reason or another would occasionally turn up fragments of domestic utensils, weapons or other articles used by the ancient pagan inhabitants of the area; and perhaps from time to time some trace of occupation by men of an even earlier period would come to light. But whether this happened or not, it was firmly believed in the Middle Ages that the foundation of Moscow went back to Biblical times. In the 17th century, for example, it was thought that the city had been established by Noah's grandson Moskh (Meshech) and his wife Kva; and the city's name was derived from the combination Moskh-Kva, giving Moskva, Moscow.

Moscow is first mentioned in the chronicles in the years 1147 and 1156 as a small frontier town in the Grand Princedom of Vladimir. A number of causes contributed to the city's rapid growth and increase in political importance. It stood at the junction of roads coming from the territory of Kiev and of Vladimir-Suzdal, and hundreds of thousands of refugees from the south and north-east sought shelter in the city during the Mongol invasion. Moreover there was for long (until the year 1261) no local princely dynasty in Moscow, which accordingly enjoyed a period of freedom from internal dissensions: a happy situation which also attracted large numbers of settlers fleeing from other parts of northern Russia.

By the end of the 13th and the beginning of the 14th century the territories of Moscow were among the most densely inhabited in the whole of Russia. The Princes now set about extending their domains, relying sometimes on the strength of their sword, sometimes on the depth of their purse. The son and grandson of Alexander Nevsky, Daniel and Yury, united to the princedom the cities of Pereyaslavl-Zalessky, Kolomna and Mozhaysk; and Ivan Kalita ("Moneybags"), the great "collector of Russian territory", cast a covetous eye on the wealth of Novgorod and fought a successful war against his powerful rival the Prince of Tver. The increasing importance of the young princedom became so evident that in 1326 the residence of the Metropolitan was transferred from the ruined city of Vladimir to Moscow, and seventy years later the Muscovites received within their walls the most revered treasure in all Russia, the icon of Our Lady of Vladimir; and with the support they now enjoyed from the Church the Princes of Moscow were able to assert their superiority over the other feudal princes of Russia.

Although Ivan Kalita's reign lasted only fifteen years (1326-1341), it was a period of remarkable success. There came over the land of Rus, records the chronicler, "a great tranquillity: the Tatars ceased their attacks on Russian soil, and Christians enjoyed relief from their grievous burdens."

In this period Moscow firmly established its claim to rank as a capital city. Its external appearance, however, did not match its importance. The area occupied by the city was only a little greater than that of the present Kremlin. The houses were unpretentious wooden structures, and the churches were likewise built of timber. In spring and autumn the narrow winding streets turned into an almost impassable morass. And all round the city, buried in luxuriant vegetation in summer and in deep snowdrifts in winter, were numbers of populous villages, externally not very different from the capital city itself.

With characteristic energy Ivan Kalita set about the rebuilding of his capital. The citadel (*kreml* or Kremlin) was surrounded by massive oak palisades, behind which gleamed the domes of the churches, now built in fair white stone. These churches have not come down to us: some of them were replaced in the late 15th and early 16th centuries by more magnificent buildings with the same names and dedications, while others were demolished without replacement.

During the regency of the Metropolitan Aleksey and the reign of Dmitry of the Don (1359-1389) the area occupied by the Kremlin was extended and the wooden palisade replaced by a stone wall. From the middle of the 14th century, and particularly after the defeat of the Mongols at the battle of Kulikovo (1380), stone building—for fortifications, monasteries and churches—became general both in Moscow and in the surrounding area.

Only a very few of the many buildings of various types erected during this period have survived. No wall painting at all has been preserved. A few icons are known, but the attribution of some of them to the Moscow school is disputed.

In many respects, therefore, our knowledge of Muscovite art of the 14th and early 15th centuries is totally lacking. Such information as we have comes from the literary sources. This is explained mainly by the fact that as Moscow developed into a large and wealthy city it increasingly attracted the rapacious attentions of the Tatars, who carried out numerous raids on the city, destroying whatever they could not carry away. Much damage was also done by fires, which were a constant hazard in the congested mass of timber houses of which mediaeval Moscow was composed. The chronicler laments that in the great fire of 1364 "the whole city was burned to the very ground"; and the number of lesser fires was beyond counting.

We know from the literary sources that in the closing years of the 14th and the early years of the 15th century the painter Theophanes the Greek, with whom we are already familiar, was working in Moscow. The paintings he did in the Kremlin churches—the Cathedral of the Nativity, the Archangel Cathedral and the Cathedral of the Annunciation—and in the *Terem*, the private apartments of the Grand Prince, have not been preserved; but he was clearly responsible for the icons in the *deesis* tier of the iconostasis in the Cathedral of the Annunciation, the finest of which are the figures of the Mother of God, John the Forerunner and the Apostle Paul.

Another artist who worked with Theophanes the Greek on the decoration of the Cathedral of the Annunciation in 1405 was Andrey Rublëv, the greatest Russian painter of the mediaeval period. His pre-eminence is taken for granted in our own day, but it was also recognised by bis contemporaries and by succeeding generations. It is surprising, therefore, to find how little information about him can be gleaned from the literary sources: even the dates of his birth and death are known only approximately.

The story of Rublëv's life as we know it today can be told very briefly. He was born in the 1360s, and was evidently a native of Moscow. While still a youth he became a monk in the Monastery of the Trinity and St Sergius (in the modern town of Zagorsk). In the nineties of the 14th century (though some scholars put the date at about 1410) he was working in Zvenigorod, in the Cathedral of the Dormition "in the Citadel" and in the Cathedral of the Nativity in the Savvino-Storozhevsky Monastery.

Evidently Rublëv's work in Zvenigorod made him known, for in 1405 we find him decorating the Cathedral of the Annunciation in Moscow along with Theophanes the Greek, and in 1408 working with Daniel the Black and "with his fellows" on the painting of frescoes and icons for the iconostasis in the Cathedral of the Dormition in Vladimir. Both of these commissions came to him from the Grand Prince, who was not accustomed to patronise unknown or obscure artists.

How Rublëv occupied his time after his return to Moscow is not known. All that we can say is that between 1410 and 1415 he probably painted the splendid icons (formerly attributed to his period in Zvenigorod) of the saviour *(Plate p. 125)*, the Archangel Michael *(Plate p. 120)* and the Apostle Paul, and that in 1411 (or, according to an alternative view, at some time during the 1420s) he painted his most famous icon, the "Trinity". At the end of the 1420s the iconostasis in the Trinity Cathedral in the Monastery of the Trinity and St Sergius was set up; and if Rublëv did not himself take part in this work it was at least carried out under his immediate supervision. It is possible also that he may have had a hand in certain other icons, the painters of which were clearly seeking to imitate his manner *(Plates pp. 126,127)*.

Rublëv died between 1427 and 1430, having at some time before his death painted the cathedral in the Andronikov Monastery in Moscow (though of this work nothing remains but a few pieces of ornament in the window niches). And it was in this nonastery, at a very advanced age and "having these many years had honourable grey hairs", that "Andrey the icon-painter" found his eternal rest. The Andronikov Monastery has now been converted into the Rublëv Museum, as a fitting tribute by posterity to this great mediaeval master.

As we have noted, Rublëv's most famous work, and indeed the most famous of all Russian icons, is his "Trinity" *(Plate p. 114)*. If we want to understand the complexity of the problems which faced the artist in this work and to appreciate the mastery with which they were solved, some preliminary explanations are required. The reader will find that the effort needed to understand this work fully will be well worth while, more particularly since most art lovers in the West are probably not familiar with this characteristically Orthodox version of the Trinity.

In mediaeval Russian painting there were three iconographical variants of the Trinity—the "Old Testament Trinity", the "Paternity" and the "New Testament Trinity". The first of these is based on a representation of three angels sitting at a table under an oak tree—the three heavenly messengers who appeared to Abraham and Sarah to tell them of the forthcoming birth of Isaac. This version is known as the "Old Testament Trinity", since the story is told in the Book of *Genesis.*

The "Paternity" shows God the Father sitting on a throne with a young, beardless Christ on his lap. Jesus is holding a sphere, and in the sphere is a white dove, representing the Holy Ghost. The "New Testament Trinity", which became popular in the 17th century, shows God the Father and Christ sitting on thrones, with the Holy Ghost hovering above them; but even in this century the more ancient "Old Testament" variant was preferred to all others. The term "Old Testament Trinity" may well strike the reader as quite inappropriate, since the doctrine of the Trinity is a dogma of Christian theology. In the Old Testament there is not, and cannot be, any mention of the Trinity, Whence, therefore, came the use of a term which can have no logical justification?

One of the basic problems facing the Church from a very early period was to combine the Old and New Testaments into an organic whole by finding a single religious conception which should link the two. For did not Christ say that he had not come to destroy the prophets but to fulfil them ? It is interesting to see how this assimilation was achieved in the Middle Ages.

Certain passages in the Old Testament prophets were interpreted as references to the Immaculate Conception, the birth of Christ, His rôle as a Messiah, and so on ; and most of the Old Testament stories were taken as symbolising events recorded in the New Testament. Among such episodes were the account of Abraham and Sarah entertaining the angels unawares and the story of Abraham's sacrifice. The New Testament parallels were not far to seek. The angels had foretold to the Patriarch the coming birth of Isaac, just as the archangel announced to the Virgin the birth of Christ. In order to test Abraham's faith God ordered him to sacrifice his son Isaac, and Isaac went like a lamb to the slaughter ; and did not Jesus do the same in accepting death on the Cross at the will of His Heavenly Father ? Such, broadly, was the reasoning of the theologians.

The artists of Byzantium and mediaeval Russia, in representing the Trinity, were in effect illustrating the Biblical text. We are told in *Genesis* that three men appeared to Abraham "in the plains of Mamre", as he "sat in the tent door in the heat of the day". Not recognising the visitors as heavenly beings, but well aware of his duty to provide hospitality, the old man bade them be seated, and gave orders for "cakes" to be baked and "a calf tender and good" to be killed for their meal. In the icons we see the angels sitting at table under an oak tree (and it will be remembered that for the icon-painters a single tree served to represent a whole forest). We see Abraham's dwelling, but the nomad's tent has become a stone-built house represented in accordance with the conventions of icon-painting. Abraham and Sarah are shown bringing cakes to their guests, and there is frequently also a young man slaughtering the calf. Some Byzantine artists included in the same composition the scene of Abraham's sacrifice.

In this treatment of the Trinity the idea of one God in three Persons was lost : the artists found no room for it in their conception of the scene. Rublëv, a man of acute intelligence and a sensitive artist, realised this omission. In painting his icon he cut out all inessential figures and narrative detail, leaving only the table, the oak-tree, the house and the pilgrims' staffs carried by the angels—an established element of the iconographical tradition—to recall the Old Testament story. The icon shows three angels with golden hair and wings sitting at a low table. Their heads are bowed, their eyes are filled with sorrow, their lips are closed. The one in the middle is pointing enquiringly at the dish containing the head of the slaughtered calf. The gesture of the angel on the left, full of mournful solemnity, seems to confirm the inevitability of the sacrifice ; and the angel on the right, as if echoing his movement, slowly lowers his hand. Everything in this picture is subordinated to the harmonious rhythm of the lines. The outlines of the angels on either side correspond exactly with the silhouette of the central figure. The angle at which the tree is bent repeats the lines of this central figure, the curve of the rock in the background matches the outline of the angel on the right, and the tiered structure of the house corresponds to the pattern formed by the body of the angel on the left.

Each of the figures in this icon represents one of the hypostases of the Trinity. This is emphasised by the different colours used in their garments—cherry red and sky blue for the angel in the middle, pinkish lilac and blue for the angel on the left, and pale green and blue for the one on the right. At the same time it is noteworthy that the garments of all three contain exactly the same shade of blue; and their faces, though there are certain barely perceptible differences between them, also show an undoubted similarity. We know with complete certainty that these three angels are indissolubly connected with one another; that they express not only their own personalities but also an essential unity. This feeling is reinforced by the composition of the icon: the three figures, sitting so closely together that their wings are touching, seem enclosed within an invisible circle which determines the whole composition.

In this work a theological conception of great complexity is given masterly artistic expression; but, as always with great art, the content of the "Trinity" has taken on characteristics which are of significance to all humanity. The arrangement of the figures in a circle, the recurrence of similar outlines, and the concentration of all glances and gestures on one object—the dish on the table *(Plate p. 117)*—emphasise the unity of thought and action which binds the three figures together. The quiet repose of the figures, the flowing rhythm of the lines, and the purity of the colours combine to create an impression of peace, tranquillity and harmony. These were precisely the qualities lacking in the world of Rublëv's day; and perhaps many of his contemporaries, as they knelt before the icon, saw in it the incarnation of the repose for which all men yearned.

Since then many centuries have passed, but for those sensitive to beauty the "Trinity" still holds its fascination. When Romain Rolland, that discerning lover of art, visited the Soviet Union in 1935 he fell under its spell. The visitors' book in the Tretyakov Gallery records his impressions: "I was delighted with the rooms filled with priceless icons. Rublëv's masterpiece will always remain in my memory as one of the most harmonious and purest of paintings."

The lessons of history had clearly demonstrated the necessity of political unification, and the battle of Kulikovo provided an instructive example of the same truth. The land of Rus was, however, still oppressed by the scourge of the feudal period—the constant internecine strife between the various princes. Thus in the 1430s there was a contest for the Muscovite throne between the Grand Prince, Vasily II, and his kinsmen Dmitry Shemyaka and Vasily Kosoy (Basil the Squint-eyed). One of the consequences of this interminably protracted struggle was the interruption of all building work in stone, for men were then too much preoccupied with other matters.

In 1462, however, Ivan III succeeded to the throne, and the situation changed completely. An adroit and far-seeing statesman and a man of boundless ambition, Ivan defeated the Princes of Yaroslav, Rostov and Beloozero, annexed Novgorod, Tver and Ryazan, and declared the Lithuanian territories which had hitherto formed part of the princedom of Kiev to belong to his ancestral patrimony. The Grand Prince of Moscow was now master of the whole of Rus, and the feudal princes were no more than great landowners who enjoyed certain special privileges. Following a practice of which history offers many examples, Ivan sought confirmation of the legitimacy of his claims in the "Tale of the Princes of Vladimir", a kind of official genealogy of the Princes of Moscow which was produced about this time. This work devotes much effort to "proving" the kinship of these princes with the Princes of Vladimir and Kiev, and tells how the Byzantine Emperor Constantine IX sent Vladimir Monomakh a royal crown, a special type of gold collar or necklace worn at coronations, and other attributes of royalty. Thereafter, says the author of the "Tale", Vladimir began to call himself Monomakh (from the Greek *monomachos* which was sometimes interpreted at this period to mean "autocrat") and "king of Great Russia". From this curious document we learn other surprising facts; for example, we are told of the bonds of kinship which linked the Princes of Moscow with such great predecessors as Constantine the Great and even the Emperor Augustus. With such a genealogical tree, there could be none to cast a doubt on the noble blood of the rulers of Moscow or on their right to the title of Tsar.

Another theory which achieved great popularity, particularly among the clergy, was the idea that Moscow was the political and spiritual heir to Byzantium (which had fallen to the Turks in 1453) and the bulwark of the Orthodox East: "Moscow the Third Rome: a fourth is not to be." In 1472, when Ivan married the Byzantine princess Sophia Palaeologus, the two-headed eagle which was the symbol of the Emperors of Byzantium became the Russian national emblem.

The unifying function of Moscow was now recognised in the terms "Muscovy" and "Muscovites" which were used in the countries of the West in referring to Russia and the Russians.

These developments had their influence on the pattern of Russian art. Attention was now concentrated on the capital city, and in particular on the Kremlin; for it had to be made evident to all that this was the residence of the all-powerful ruler of these northern territories. But first, since the Kremlin still retained its function as a fortress, its defences—which by the end of the 15th century were somewhat dilapidated and ill adapted to the new methods of warfare based on the use of fire-arms—had to be reconstructed in accordance with the latest techniques of fortification.

At this period the Italians had the greatest reputation as builders, and Italian architects and craftsmen were therefore invited to work in Moscow. Men like Fioravanti, Solari, Ruffo and Alevisio were thus able to make use of Italian experience in this field for the creation of an architectural ensemble which gave expression to distinctively Russian traditions and styles.

The builders starded with the walls and towers of the Kremlin, erecting tall massive ramparts with three tiers of apertures from which fire could be directed against the enemy. A network of passages and chambers was contrived within the thickness of the walls, and underground tunnels were driven at suitable places to provide listening posts from which a watch could be kept on enemy attempts to undermine the defences. In addition the approaches to the fortress were defended on one side by the River Moskva and on the other by the Neglinnaya, and the two rivers were later joined by a moat. It was not surprising, therefore, that foreign ambassadors and other visitors described the Kremlin as one of the strongest fortresses in Europe. The main entrance was at the Frolovsky Tower (renamed the Spassky Tower in the 17th century, when the spire with its clocks was added) *(Plate p. 97 left)*. The Frolovsky Gate led into Cathedral Square, where building was carried on simultaneously with the work on the fortifications.

Between 1475 and 1479 the Cathedral of the Dormition *(Plate p. 101)* was built by the Bologna architect Ridolfo Fioravanti, who was given the name of Aristotele "by reason of his great skill at the art". The building of the cathedral had begun before Fioravanti arrived in Russia; but evidently the builders—whose names are recorded as Myshkin and Krivtsov—were of no great competence. The mortar they used was of insufficient strength, so that their work could not withstand "an earthquake which shook the city of Moscow"; and the building, which had almost reached roof level, collapsed. There soon arose in its place a new Cathedral of the Dormition, the model for which was provided by the cathedral of the same name in Vladimir. Fioravanti, however, was too good an architect to confine himself to a slavish copy of his model. Features which recall the ancient shrine of Vladimir are the plan, the stone walls (the light vaulting, however, being of brick), the subdivision of the external wall surfaces, the vaulted roof, the massive group of five domes, the narrow slit-like windows, the splayed doorways and the blind arcades which run round the whole building half-way up the walls. (The painting on the walls above the doorways dates from the 17th century) *(Plate p. 99)*. Novel features were the flattened apses, the projecting walls to the north and south of the apses, and the high plinth (now no longer visible, since the foundations of the cathedral are now considerably below ground level). The structural techniques also show new features−the use of specially made bricks, iron tierods, and so on.

The interior of the cathedral *(Plate p. 98)* is light and spacious. The chancel and the altar rails (which were concealed by the tall iconostasis built in the 17th century) were covered with brightly coloured frescoes. The rest of the cathedral was not painted until 1544. Of the original paintings, however, only a few fragments have survived, most of those now visible having been repainted in the middle of the 17th century. If we imagine the church as it once was, with the silver lustres hanging from the vaulting, the gold and silver vessels and the icons in their sumptuous frames, glittering with precious stones, we can understand the impression it created on contemporaries: "A church marvellous in size and height, in brightness and resonance, and of wondrous spaciousness", it was called by the proud citizens of Moscow.

And indeed the Cathedral of the Dormition was intended to convey an impression of magnificence. In those days it was the most important public building in the Kremlin, the place where solemn ceremonies were held, where Grand Princes and Tsars were crowned. Here also was the burial vault of the Metropolitan, and later of the Patriarch.

In the 1480s craftsmen from Pskov reconstructed the Cathedral of the Annunciation, originally built in the 14th century, in a style which incorporated features from the architecture of Vladimir and Pskov. The original church, a small building with three domes, had now become the court church ; and accordingly in 1564 galleries containing four small chapels were built round three sides and the number of domes was increased to nine.

The third of the main churches in the Kremlin *(Plate p. 100)*, the Archangel Cathedral, was rebuilt later than the others. Ivan III did not live to see it, for it was not completed until after his death, in 1509. The Italian master builder Aleviz Novy, "Alevisio the Second", allowed himself a good deal of liberty with the traditions of Russian architecture. The double row of windows and the wide cornice which runs round the church half-way up the walls give it the appearance of a two-storied building. A similar cornice cuts off the *zakomary*, the rounded pediments at the top of the gables, from the main structure of the wall; and the carved scallop-shell mouldings which cover their whole surface give the *zakomary* themselves a purely decorative significance. The mouldings in the *zakomary*, the cornices, the pilasters, the decoration of the external walls (with panels in the upper part and blind arcades in the lower), the loggia on the west front and the doorways framed in splendid carved ornament in the style of the late Italian Renaissance make the Archangel Cathedral, in spite of the traditional plan and the group of five domes, the least Russian in spirit of all the buildings erected in the Kremlin at this period. We have only to think of it without the domes and we are reminded at once of a north Italian *palazzo*.

Of the palace buildings belonging to the reign of Ivan III the only one that has survived is the Granovitaya Palata, the Palace of Facets, built by Pietro Antonio Solari and Marco Ruffo in 1487-1491. It has a double row of windows and an almost flat roof, and above a ground floor of undecorated stonework is the façade of rusticated stone from which the palace takes its name. The interior is reminiscent of the Vladychnaya Palata in Novgorod, with a massive square pier in the centre supporting the groined vault *(Plates pp. 102, 103)*. The pier is decorated with carved stone ornament, and it is thought that originally the walls were similarly carved. The walls were decorated with painting in the reign of Boris Godunov (1598-1605), but although the painting was renewed in the 17th century none of it has survived. The paintings we see today were done by artists from Palekh in 1882.

The Palace of Facets was the first public building of a secular character to be built in Muscovite Russia. Here the Princes and Tsars held counsel with their boyars, received foreign ambassadors and gave great feasts. On the occasion of a feast tables and benches were set out round the walls, and on a dais a special table was laid for the Muscovite ruler himself. Round the central pier was erected a tiered display stand, on which were exhibited great numbers of gold and silver vessels of every shape and size — cups, goblets, pitchers, and boat-shaped ladles or scoops with long curved handles. Some were no bigger than a modern coffee cup, others were so large that, in the words of Peter Petrey of Erlesund, "ducks and geese could swim in them".

The tallest structure in the Kremlin, and indeed in the whole of the mediaeval city, was the towerlike church and belfry dedicated to St John Climacus. Because of its height it was also used as a watchtower. This unusual church was built between 1505 and 1508 by the architect Bon Fryazin in place of a 14th century church of the same name. The 260 feet high tower was popularly known as "Ivan the Great", and the Cathedral Square became the Ivanovsky Square.

The building operations in the Kremlin begun during the reign of Ivan III continued in the reign of his son Vasily III. By the year 1516 the citadel of the Grand Princes of Moscow had taken on an appearance not very different from that familiar to us in later centuries. There were the same massive battlemented walls and the same towers (though still with squat tent roofs — the tall spires we see today were not built until the 17th century); and within the ramparts rose the white walls of the churches, surmounted by the warm golden glow of their domes. At the gates the guards stood vigilant watch, and round the walls the sentries kept up their ceaseless pacing, disturbing the silence of the night with their watchwords. Within the triangle formed by the Moskva, the Neglinnaya and the moat which joined the two rivers, the Kremlin towered over the timber-built town below, casting the reflections of its massive red and white walls on the placid water. The citadel was linked with the bustling settlement which surrounded it by a number of chain drawbridges and one stone bridge; and on every side the suburbs of the town straggled out into the countryside to disappear in the distant haze.

Building continued in the Kremlin during the 16th century: streets and squares, churches and even monasteries, mansions for the Prince, the Metropolitan, the boyars, store-rooms and domestic offices. "In its extent the citadel almost resembles a city," wrote Baron Herberstein, the Emperor's ambassador in Moscow in the reign of Vasily III.

In Moscow itself there was no lack of work for builders, and craftsmen skilled in every trade were summoned from all over Russia to play their part in the Tsar's building programme. In the 1580s a special department, the Masonry Board, was established to take charge of all government building. Moreover during the struggle for the unification of the country great quantities of works of art of all kinds—icons, bone and wood carving, objects of gold and silver, and so on—were brought to Moscow from the old capitals of the feudal apanages. The flow of such material to Moscow was intensified during the reign of Ivan the Terrible (1547-1584), when it was brought in almost by the cart-load. All these factors together led to a situation in which the work of the architects, painters and other craftsmen of the 16th century gradually tended to lose the distinguishing characteristics of the local schools, which merged with the school of Moscow to produce a unified stylistic amalgam. There were, of course, still some local features: thus if we consider certain churches in the Pokrovsky Monastery in Suzdal or the Cathedral of the Dormition *(Plate p. 80)* in the citadel of Rostov *(Plate p. 77)* we recognise the blind arcades as a reminiscence of an ancient local tradition. Nevertheless the features which immediately strike us in these and other 16th century buildings are the elements common to them all which reflect the accepted style of the period.

Among the works of fortification built in Moscow in this period mention must be made of the walls and towers of the old Kitay-Gorod, built by Petrok Maly between 1534 and 1538. These fortifications were now of vital importance to the city, for in the event of a siege of any duration the Kremlin could no longer have accommodated the greatly enlarged population of Moscow. The new fortifications, like those of the Kremlin, were designed for the new conditions of warfare based on the use of fire-arms.

The Kitay-Gorod was the business and commercial quarter of Moscow in this period, densely packed with shops and craftsmen's workshops. It was in this area that Ivan the Terrible later built the first timber Gostinny Dvor (bazaar). The name of the Kitay-Gorod is usually derived from the Russian name for China *(Kitay)*, but in fact there is no basis for this etymology. *Kitay* comes from an old Russian word meaning "wattle", and we have already noted that the word for "town,,, *gorod*, originally meant a fortress. A year before the erection of the stone wall round the Kitay-Gorod we find the following passage in the chronicles: "A fortress was built in Moscow, made of earth; ... most skilfully was it constructed... Slender branches were woven round a stout log; within this, earth was built up and ... firmly established ... And they gave the fortress the name of Kitay. "And so the name which at first sight appears so exotic finds a simple and natural explanation.

As we have seen, the monasteries played an important part in the defence of the country. Of those in the area round Moscow the most important are the Novodevichy and the Monastery of the Trinity and St Sergius.

The Novodevichy Monastery *(Plates pp. 134, 135)* was built in 1524-25 by Vasily III in fulfilment of a vow he had taken in 1514, before undertaking a campaign against Smolensk; and accordingly the principal church in the monastery − a five-domed structure built in brick with stone details, following a typical 16th century pattern − was dedicated to the icon of Our Lady of Smolensk *(Plate p. 136)*. The monastery was built at a bend in the River Moskva, at a point where there were three crossings, leading respectively to Dorogomilovo, Krymsky Brod and the Vorobyëvy Gory ("Sparrow Hills").

The site selected for this new monastery was a clear indication of its strategic importance; and we are reminded of this at once by the great machicolated walls and towers, decked out though they now are with a tracery of stone ornament added in the 17th century. Indeed this decoration, like the airy openwork silhouette of the belfry, the elegant red and white refectory church, and the church above the entrance gateway with its decorative domes and carved scallop-shells – all built in the 17th century in the style known as "Naryshkin baroque" – merely serves to emphasise the massive bulk of the old 16th century fortifications.

The Monastery of the Trinity and St Sergius also stood on one of the approaches to Moscow. Founded by Sergy Radonezhsky in the middle of the 14th century and originally built in timber, it was burned down by the Tatars in 1408. It was then rebuilt, again in timber – of which there was an abundant supply in the dense forests which stretched for many miles round the monastery. For several decades the only stone building here was the Cathedral of the Trinity (1422). It was not until 1469 that a second stone building was erected, the refectory church (reconstructed in the 17th century); then, eight years later, craftsmen from Pskov built in brick the small single-domed Church of the Holy Ghost *(Plate p. 137)*.

It might be thought that the bitter experience of the preceding hundred and fifty years had shown the prime importance of having secure fortifications. Yet a beginning was not made until 1540, and even then there was no great air of haste: the stone ramparts which replaced the old timber palisades were fully ten years in the building. Once built, however, the stout battlemented walls and massive towers with their squat tent roofs served their purpose well. In 1608, for example, in the evil days of the *Samozvanshchina,* the "Time of the Impostors" or Time of Troubles – the "Ruin of Moscow", as the old historians called it – the Monastery of St Sergius successfully withstood many months of siege by Polish and Lithuanian forces.

During this period church building continued actively, as in the past. Perhaps the most important monastery church dating from this time is the Cathedral of the Dormition in the Monastery of the Trinity and St Sergius, which was begun in 1559, in the reign of Ivan the Terrible, but not completed until 26 years later. Built in brick, with a vaulted roof, five domes and five apses – the present hipped roof with massive onion domes dates from a later period – it somewhat resembled the Cathedral of the Dormition in the Kremlin. Thus both in plan and in architectural form the Cathedral of the Dormition in St Sergius was a wholly traditional building.

A very distinctive type of church which now made its appearance, however, was the "tower church" with its striking tent roof. One of the first of these was the Church of the Ascension built in 1530-32 in the village of Kolomenskoe, an estate belonging to the Grand Prince in the countryside near Moscow *(Plate p. 139)*.

Apart from the fact that the Kolomenskoe church is built in brick with stone detailing in the normal 16th century manner, the building represents a striking departure from the accepted standards of stone-built church architecture, with the tiered structure of its tower, the octagonal tent roof surmounted by a small lantern and cupola, the high basement with a gallery and steps running down to ground level, and the absence of an apse, a feature hitherto included in all stone-built churches. "Made in

the image of a church built in wood," the people of Moscow very rightly decided; and they added, struck with admiration at the builders' skill: "Such a church had never been seen in Russia before."

No doubt the admiration of contemporaries for the church at Kolomenskoe encouraged the architects of the day to further efforts in the same direction. Numbers of other tower churches were now built, in designs of increasing complexity. In the Church of the Decollation of St John the Forerunner (1547) in the village of Dyakovo, on the outskirts of Moscow, the central tower is surrounded by four smaller corner towers; and the Cathedral of the Protection of the Virgin "on the Moat", in Red Square in Moscow, has no fewer than nine towers.

Few people will recognise this interesting building under its original name, but it is widely known as the Cathedral of St Basil the Blessed. Basil the Blessed was a *yurodivy*, a "witless one", who apparently died in Moscow in 1552, the year of the capture of Kazan. He had become famous for his fearless denunciation of the cruelties of Ivan the Terrible—for in those days it was thought that the simpleminded enjoyed the special favour of God and that even the Tsar could not compel them to keep silent. Basil was buried in the churchyard of the Trinity Church, which stood on the site later to be occupied by the Church of the Protection. He was canonised soon after his death, and when the cathedral was built one of the internal chapels was dedicated to him; but the saint was so popular in Moscow that the whole cathedral came to be known as the church of Basil the Blessed *(Plate p. 138)*.

The Church of the Protection was built in fulfilment of a vow. In mediaeval Russia important events were not commemorated by the erection of monuments but by the building of churches; and the new cathedral was built to celebrate the capture of Kazan from the Tatars. Kazan fell on 1st October 1552, on the feast of the Protection of the Virgin, and this determined the dedication of the cathedral.

The chronicler gives a concise description of the architecture of the cathedral in these words: "A church was built of most wondrous form, having nine altars of various appearance and form erected on a single base". And indeed, as we can see today, the nine towers rise from a single platform, the central tower having a tent roof with a small bulbous dome, the others onion-shaped domes ribbed and fluted in varying patterns, so that no one of the towers is exactly similar to any of the others. The different towers are linked by a gallery with with staircases and flights of steps which runs round the entire building. (The flights of steps, the galleries and the belfries were added in the 17th century). Here and there the brick walls are relieved by the gleam of coloured tiles; the foundations, the basement and the architectural details are in stone.

According to an old legend Ivan the Terrible caused the builders of the cathedral, Barma and Posnik, to be blinded so that they should never build another church to compare with it. Whether true or not, this grisly tradition does at any rate show the impression made on contemporaries by the fantastic architecture of St Basil the Blessed.

In the reigns of Ivan the Terrible's successors, Fëdor Ivanovich and Boris Godunov, building continued in the principal cities of Russia. In the 1590s Fëdor Kon built the citadel of Smolensk. In Moscow two further defensive lines were constructed, the "White City" and the "Earthen City", and the dominance of the Kremlin was still further enhanced by the heightening of the bell-tower of Ivan the Great (1600). The appearance of the streets of Moscow was also now transformed. The citizens were no longer exposed to the risk, in rainy weather, of sinking up to their knees in mud; the streets in the centre of the town were paved with wood, and even in the lesser streets planks were provided on which pedestrians could pass safely over the mud and slush. The people of Moscow were sure that there was no fairer city in all Russia : "Majestic and beautiful is this mighty city" — such was the proud boast of its citizens.

To bring to life the vanished world of the Middle Ages on the basis of the fragments which have survived from the past is a wellnigh impossible task. Wars, ignorance and indifference, and the ruthless destruction of antiquities have caused irreparable loss and damage. Thus our knowledge of the monumental painting of the 16th century depends mainly on descriptions by contemporaries, together with a few fragments of áctual painting which have miraculously survived. We must now consider what account can be given of this painting on the basis of the scanty material available to us.

The artists now tended to make increasing use of Old Testament subjects drawn from various edifying collections and from the lives of Russian saints. No definite canons had yet been laid down for these subjects, and the nature of the themes made it possible for the artists to introduce all kinds of lively and entertaining details. The spirit of the times was expressed in the russifying of the Gospel stories : thus a publican and a Pharisee are shown praying in front of an icon of the Saviour, the miracle of the healing of the man born blind takes place in a single-domed Russian church, and so on. In church paintings dating from the reign of Ivan the Terrible we can detect a preference for apocalyptic themes, understandable enough in that period of trial and tribulation. The Tsar's lowering glance drove away the luminous images created by Andrey Rublëv, Dionysius and their followers; in their place representations of the Last Judgment painted detailed pictures of the torments of Hell (as in churches in the Aleksandrova Sloboda, Yaroslavl and Solvychegodsk), and the churches of the 16th century became tenanted by hosts of winged demons.

In the reign of Ivan IV the Golden Room in the Kremlin Palace was decorated with painting, and in Boris Godunov's the Palace of Facets. We know what these paintings were like from a description by the 17th century artist Ushakov, who was given the task of restoring them. From Ushakov's account it is clear that the paintings in both of these palaces were conceived for a particular purpose : in the phrase of a student of early Russian art, "the figures and incidents depicted were used to present certain specific ideas". The paintings were intended as a celebration of the kingdom of Russia, a glorification of the Grand Princes and Tsars and of the policies they pursued.

In this connection it is interesting to recall a curious incident which took place in 1551. In that year a council of Church leaders, the Stoglav or "Hundred-headed Assembly[1]", was held in Moscow, presided over by Ivan the Terrible himself. The assembly was concerned not only with ecclesiastical matters but with questions relating to art—what themes artists should handle and how they should represent them. The Tsar asked, for example, whether the figures of ordinary mortals who were still alive could appear on icons along with the figures of saints. The Church fathers replied that this had been the practice in ancient times and cited examples, adding that "in icons of the Day of Judgment...

---

[1] The term "hundred-headed" derives from the fact that the decisions of the assembly were later published in a collection which contained a hundred "heads" or chapters.

there appear the figures not only of saints but of unbelievers." Although the question was direct enough, the reply was exceedingly evasive. Nevertheless it was sufficient; for within a few years there appeared the painting of the "Great Entrance" in the church of the Monastery of Sviyazhsk, which included figures of Ivan IV and Germanus, abbot of the monastery, and the icon of "The Church Militant" (originally known as "The Blessed Army of the Heavenly King"), in which, amid angels and saints, we again see the figure of the overweeningly ambitious Tsar. The icon shows the victorious host advancing in three columns along the banks of a river winding between densely wooded hills *(Plates pp. 130-133)*. Behind them is the city of Kazan, in flames, and in front is the Heavenly City of Jerusalem. At the gates of Jerusalem are the Virgin and Child, and angels are crowning the victors with golden crowns which they have received from the hands of Jesus. At the head of the army is the Archangel Michael, galloping along on a winged horse and pointing to the walls of Jerusalem, as if drawing attention to the celestial bliss which lies so close at hand. Behind him is the youthful commander of the army, Tsar Ivan, riding at a steady pace and looking round at the ranks of warriors behind him, while angels crown him with a golden crown.

The icon was painted to commemorate the capture of Kazan. But why, one may well ask, do the warriors include a gigantic figure of Constantine the Great carrying a cross, as well as the three princes, Vladimir, Boris and Gleb? What connection can this event which took place in the year 1552 have with a 4th century Greek Emperor and these 11th century Russian princes? There is, of course, no connection at all. The figures are included to emphasise certain historical parallels: Constantine contended with heretics, Vladimir baptised the heathen, Ivan IV converted Mohammedans to the Orthodox faith. Moreover the icon presents in pictorial form the idea, so dear to the heart of the rulers of Moscow since the time of Ivan's grandfather, of a direct line of succession running from Constantine to Vladimir, and from Vladimir to Ivan IV. And finally Boris and Gleb appear on the icon as the patron saints of the Russian army.

The trends we have noted in the painting in the Kremlin palaces and in the icon of the "Church Militant" were so strongly entrenched in this period that they are found even in works of applied art. Of particular interest from this point of view are the carved wooden reliefs on Ivan the Terrible's throne in the Cathedral of the Dormition in the Kremlin. The throne stands under a tent-shaped wooden canopy borne on four carved columns, which in turn rest on four symbolic animals. The sides of the throne are decorated with carvings of scenes, part historical, part apocryphal, showing the life and achievements of Vladimir Monomakh, from his legendary campaigns in Thrace to the equally fantastic story of his receiving the Imperial regalia from Byzantium. "Moscow, the Third Rome": the object of all this is transparently clear, particularly if we recall that the throne was made in 1551, at the very time when Ivan the Terrible was so insistent in seeking confirmation of his royal authority.

Ivan IV's reign, full of storm and stress as it was, also provided the conditions for the emergence of other and very different trends. It was a time of intense intellectual activity, when men with a bent for observation, and for drawing deductions from what they observed, sought to distinguish the elements of good and evil in human life and to establish their causes. The evil, of course, was evident at every turn; and the best minds of the day thought that once the distempers of society had been exposed it was possible to point to the means of cure. This feeling gave birth to a great body of moralising literature

—of what might, in modern terms, be called propaganda. This usually took the form of stories or parables, for the 16th century was inordinately fond of the language of allegory—and in any event there were dangers about saying certain things directly. The life and behaviour of the clergy were attracting increasing attention from the enlightened thinkers of the 16th century: in particular, men remarked on the enormous increase in the wealth of the Church and on its ambition to play a part in the government of the country. To make matters worse, although there were among the clergy men of culture and intelligence whose life was governed by the strictest rules of morality, the middle and lower clergy, particularly the monks, fell far short of these standards, being noted for their persistent drunkenness and debauchery, their greed and their hypocrisy.

Surprising as it may seem, the reaction against such conditions was sometimes expressed in the works of the icon-painters. As instances of this we may take the icons of the "Vision of the Ladder" and the "Parable of the Lame Man and the Blind Man" (both in the Russian Museum).

The "Vision of the Ladder" is associated with the name of a learned monk of the 7th century, John Climacus, who was at one time abbot of the famous monastery on Mount Sinai. He received the name John Climacus, John of the Ladder, from the book he wrote called the "Ladder to Paradise"—a guide to the monastic life, which he saw as a steady ascent up the ladder of self-improvement. In the icon we see on the left the saintly author reading his work to the assembled brethren, and on the right, as if in illustration of his words, a ladder leading up from earth to Heaven, to the very gates of Paradise. At the entrance to Paradise we see Christ, the Virgin, and St John the Forerunner, along with angels; and close by, on elegantly patterned clouds, are a host of the blessed. A number of monks are engaged in climbing up the ladder. Only one of them has reached the top, and round his head glows a golden nimbus. The rest are either clinging to the lowest rungs or, having progressed hafl-way up, have missed their footing and, to the delight of the demons who are hovering nearby, are falling into the yawning mouth of Hell which lies below, where the rulers of the underworld, Pluto Proserpine, with all their hellish train, are awaiting their prey. The moral is so obvious that no further commentary is required.

The interpretation of the "Parable of the Lame Man and the Blind Man" is more complex (Plate p. 129). We see two beggars, a lame man and a blind man, sitting at the gates of a garden: the owner of the garden, Christ, has taken pity on them and set them to watch over his property. But the wretched pair feel no sense of gratitude, and we see the blind man taking the lame man on his shoulders so that he can pluck the fruit from the trees. For this offence they are driven from the garden and, pursued by the Archangel Michael with his spear, fall straight into Hell. The blind man and the lame man are the unrighteous pastors whose duty it was to preserve the teachings of Christ in their purity—the fruits of the heavenly garden—but who had been blind and deaf to the Word of God and lame in performing the duties laid upon them. Forgetful of all spiritual blessings, they are concerned only to amass the good things of this world. There is a direct allusion here to the Church's pursuit of worldly riches, its disregard of the principles of the Gospel teaching; and the icon is thus a direct expression of the ideas which were exercising Russian society in this period.

The range of subject matter of the icons of the 16th century was enormously enlarged in comparison with earlier periods. Themes such as "In Thee rejoiceth every creature" and "Let everything that has breath praise the Lord" become increasingly frequent. The denizens of Heaven are surrounded by accurate representations of plants, flowers and trees, and a variety of creatures—furred, feathered or clad with scales—such as have never existed on land or in the sea. It is as if the artists had noticed for the first time that the world was not inhabited solely by saints and incorporeal beings. It is significant that icons devoted to the lives of saints—which had occurred since the 14th century but had been relatively rare—should now begin to appear in considerable number. In these works the centre of the icon is occupied by a particular figure or figures, while round the edge is a series of square panels representing scenes from the life of the principal character. These marginal pictures are usually most entertaining and full of fascinating detail from everyday life. Moreover, in accordance with a trend which we have already noted as typical of the period, the local colour in these scenes is very Russian : the action takes place in Russian churches or palaces, the Biblical characters are frequently clad in the garb of Russian Tsars or boyars, and so on *(Plate p. 67)*.

The world of everyday reality is even more frequently represented in the miniatures than in the icons. The miniaturist enjoyed more freedom in depicting this world than the icon-painter, for he was less closely bound by traditional models: indeed, it was not easy to find models for the themes with which the miniaturist was concerned.

Among the miniatures which have survived from this period—and in this respect the miniatures have been more fortunate than the frescoes of the 16th century—the most interesting are those in the "Illustrated Collection of Chronicles" and in various lives of saints.

The "Illustrated Collection", a work commissioned by the Tsar himself, was first conceived in the 1550s and brought to completion in the 1570s. It contained all the old chronicles of the various feudal princedoms, including in particular the Princedom of Moscow, and comprehended the whole history of the world as it was then understood, from the Book of *Genesis* to the events of the 16th century. As it has come down to us, the work consists of six volumes devoted to the history of Russia and contains something like 10,000 miniatures on a great variety of subjects, which tell us a great deal about mediaeval weapons, domestic equipment, dress, and many other aspects of mediaeval life.

Many of these pictures of everyday life are found illustrating the lives of Russian saints. They show us the icon-painter at work, the monastery school, and a great variety of people going about their everyday occupations—bakers, carpenters, ploughmen, woodmen, and so on—and thus form a source of inestimable value for the social historian. There are also many pictures of quite a different type—idyllic scenes which express a deep love for the unpretentious beauties of the countryside of northern Russia. We see, for example, hermits building timber huts on the fringe of a forest, or monks engaged in earnest conversation as they stroll under an overhanging canopy of birches or firs or along the banks of a placid stream.

In the 1550s, too, following the example shown by Ivan Fëdorov, deacon of the Church of St Nicholas in the Kremlin, come the first printed books, and with them the technique of woodcut illustrations. This technique was used for headings and tailpieces, ornamental frames round the pages, and portraits of the authors—thus taking over the whole of the field which had formerly belonged to the miniaturist. There is one exception to this: woodcuts are rarely used in the 16th century to illustrate the text, though in the following century they are widely employed for this purpose. The popularity of the woodcut is hardly surprising, for it was very much quicker to engrave a picture on a block of wood, coat it with black ink and print it than to paint a picture with fine brushes on parchment—quite apart from the fact that the same block could be used to produce a large number of prints. Although it took several decades to complete the change-over, the introduction of printing meant the end of the ancient art of miniature-painting.

Surprising though it may seem, the development of the woodcut spelt the ruin of the whole of the representational art of the Middle Ages; for—slowly, perhaps, but none the less surely—it undermined the whole foundations of this art. Woodcuts, even when they depicted a particular subject or incident, were, after all, no more than book illustrations, and the prescriptions of the Church ceased to apply. Moreover the first woodcuts, like the whole technique of engraving on wood, came to Russia from the West, where the problems now presenting themselves to Russian artists had long since been solved. It was no accident, therefore, that it was the wood-engraver rather than the painter who first concerned himself in Russia with such questions as the proper representation of space or the anatomically accurate depiction of the human figure; no accident that it was the woodcuts rather than the icons which first showed the new trend, in which ordinary men and women began to replace the saints, and the scenes in which they appeared began to break free from the rules laid down by the Church. Thus the Russian woodcut of the 16th century leads directly into the art of the 17th century, the final century of the older Russia, with all its new, complex and conflicting problems.

VI The Seventeenth century

The study of Russian art has made great strides in the years since the second world war. During these years many works by Russian artists and craftsmen have been collected, restored and carefully studied, and numerous books and articles have been published which throw fresh light on the history of Russian art. This is particularly true of mediaeval art, and it is also true of 18th century art. In these fields impressive progress has been made. All over Russia, in old churches and local museums, are large numbers of important works which are now being systematically collected and studied and are steadily supplementing the resources of the great museums. Much new light has also been thrown on the art of the 17th century, so that we are now in a position to define more accurately its particular aesthetic qualities.

In Russia the 17th century began with the stormy period known as the Time of Troubles, which had far-reaching effects on the economic and political, and consequently also on the spiritual, life of Russian society. After the death of Ivan the Terrible and the reign of Boris Godunov the country suffered further afflictions in the form of a disastrous harvest and a severe famine throughout the whole of Russia. Popular discontent led to risings against the boyars and landowners, and many peasants absconded from the estates to which they were bound. These stirrings of revolt in turn led the ruling classes of feudal society to enter into an agreement with the Poles under which they gained possession of Moscow, while the Swedes occupied the northern territories of Russia.

The famine, destruction and pillaging which accompanied this foreign occupation threatened the very existence of the kingdom, and life in the cities came almost to a standstill. In this fateful hour, however, there developed a patriotic movement for the re-establishment of Russian independence and the expulsion of the foreign oppressors. The heroes of this movement were Kuzma Minin and Dmitry Pozharsky, who led a national rising against the enemy and succeeded in driving out the occupying forces and restoring some degree of order in the country; and in 1713 the young Michael Romanov, the founder of the last dynasty to rule over Russia, was elected Tsar.

The election of a Tsar did not, however, mean that the country's difficulties were over. The turmoil of the early years of the century had far-reaching consequences and set powerful social forces in motion. These years of constant struggle against internal troubles and external enemies formed the character of the Russian people, strengthening their national awareness and their consciousness of their own strength.

An event of first-rate importance during this period was the union of the Ukraine with Russia, which increased the extent and enhanced the importance of the kingdom. Meanwhile the Russians were actively engaged in winning Siberia and the northern territories, developing their trade, building ships and sending a variety of expeditions to the East — leading to the discovery of Kamchatka, the Kuriles, the straits between Asia and America, etc.

The growing might of Muscovy was now increasingly borne in on the countries of the West. In the 17th century relationships between Russia and these countries became closer, and trading links were established with many other countries, ranging as far afield as India and the distant land of China.

Wars, social unrest, schism within the Church, peasant risings, calamitous destruction and the rapid rebirth of new towns from the ashes of the old: this was the pattern of the century, which gave a special vigour and dynamism to the life of Russia in this period. Entirely new impulses made themselves felt in the social framework which had persisted throughout so many centuries, giving fresh direction to many aspects of Russian life.

Life, indeed, was not easy for the Russians of the 17th century. The age-old struggle to wrest a living from nature, the constant fight against the oppressions of the Tsars and boyars, and the wars with the foreign aggressors who sought to occupy the soil of Russia — all these things strengthened the Russian character and gave it a distinctive stamp. The difficulties with which the Russian people had perpetually to contend developed a characteristic shrewdness and spirit of enterprise, a courage which shrank from nothing, and an indefatigable energy. In spite of all their tribulations the people of Russia preserved their optimism, their independence and their belief in the beauty of the world which surrounded them. And these characteristics inevitably influenced their art: the complex, troubled and contradictory history of the 17th century was faithfully reflected in the work of both folk and professional artists, which was as complex and variable as the life of the period which it portrayed.

The art of the 17th century has been the subject of very varying judgments by Russian critics. Some writers regard it as the time of flowering of the older Russian art; others as a period of decline which saw "the dying out of all the arts of ancient Russia". These are extreme views, reflecting the aesthetic principles of particular scholars. But in our own day, in the light of intensive study of the culture of the period and detailed examination of its painting, graphic art and architecture, it is possible to make a profounder and more objective assessment of 17th century Russian art and to recognise both its qualities and its defects; and we can now identify more clearly the new features which give so much of the work of this period its own particular charm.

The 17th century surpassed all earlier periods in the abundance and magnificence of the architecture it produced and in the unprecedented development of monumental painting of remarkable originality and richness of form. We can at once distinguish two opposing trends in the art of this century. On the one hand it was still under the influence of the old mediaeval traditions; on the other it was developing realistic tendencies which were entirely new. In this sense the culture of the period is clearly transitional, though at the same time it has a distinctive character of its own, which is clearly recognisable in the work it produced. The development of 17th century art is commonly referred to as a process of "secularisation"; and this term accurately expresses the declining influence of Church dogma and the assertion of lay

influences which were more closely in touch with the circumstances of everyday life. This is true of Russian culture as a whole, and of all the various genres of figurative art. It is very necessary to understand this process, since it gives us an essential insight into the character of Russian art in this period and the pattern of its development. This secularisation becomes particularly evident in the second half of the century.

The occupation of Moscow by the Poles led to the destruction and desecration of its numerous churches. The old timber-built city suffered heavy damage; large areas were burned down, and many streets and squares were left abandoned and desolate. "Then the tall houses of the city, resplendent with many beauties, were destroyed," records the chronicler; "everything was consumed by fire, and all the churches with their fair domes were utterly brought to ruin by the foul hands of the enemy." The same fate befell other towns which lay in the path of the invaders. Then the upsurge of national feeling which followed the Time of Troubles led to vigorous building activity throughout the country and particularly, of course, in the capital. This rebuilding completely altered the appearance of many towns: new centres were created, whole layouts were changed, new fortifications were built and numbers of new religious and secular buildings were erected.

All this new building was strictly controlled. A special "Masonry Board" was established to take charge of the whole building programme, arrangements were made for the training of architects and builders, a standard size of brick was prescribed, and so on. All this ensured that the rebuilding was carried out in a properly planned and organised way and was recognised as an enterprise of supreme national importance. The chaotic huddle of building which had been characteristic of earlier towns now began to disappear, and the wider problems of town planning received consideration for the first time and were solved in ways which took account of the requirements of the whole architectural complex. Much of the new building was in stone and brick — another indication of the general improvement in the standard of architecture.

The rich store of experience built up by each successive generation of builders was now handed on to the next. We know the names of many of the leading architects of the 17th century − Antip Konstantinov, Bazhen Ogurtsov, the Startsev brothers, Averky Mokeev, Pavel Potekhin, Yakov Bukhvostov and many others − whose work gives evidence of remarkable talent and professional skill.

A characteristic feature of 17th century architecture is the emergence of local schools − in Moscow, Ryazan, Yaroslavl, Rostov, Suzdal and other towns − each with its own distinctive style, its own individual conception of architectural form. Although all these schools had a certain community of style and technique, each of them had its own specific characteristics. In spite of these local variations, however, the distinctive features which are common to all 17th century architecture are readily perceptible and can be recognised at a glance.

The religious buildings of the early years of the century show little trace of novelty. The planning and decoration of the churches is very similar to that of earlier buildings. As examples of the work of this period we may take the Church of the Protection of the Virgin in Rubtsovo (1626) and the Church of St Nicholas in Yaroslavl (1621), in both of which the general composition and decoration are completely traditional. In these early years of the century we see a continuation of the trend away from the tent roof *(shatër)*.

In the second quarter of the century new features begin to assert themselves, and the distinctive features of 17th century architecture begin to take shape. The tendency is now towards an assymetric layout: the main structure of the church is surrounded by a whole range of chapels, porches, staircases, galleries, passages, flights of steps, and so on, creating an effect of great variety and picturesqueness. Whereas earlier churches had as a rule formed a complete architectural whole, often standing by itself, the new buildings bore a much closer spatial relationship to their surroundings. The accent was now laid on the three-dimensional plastic quality of the architecture, and the buildings of the period are remarkable for their complex decorative structure and striking effect.

We may take as an example the Church of the Trinity in Nikitniki, Moscow, built between 1623 and 1653. The high square tower with its domes, the two chapels, the porch and the bell-tower combine to produce a building of great picturesque effect: an effect which is enhanced by the *kokoshniki* (decorative gable-heads), the pairs of colonnettes, the brick mouldings and the use of polychrome decoration.

Another typical building of this period is the Church of the Prophet Elijah in Yaroslavl (1647-50) *(Plate p. 176)*, a five-domed structure to which a number of chapels, flights of steps and porches are annexed. The octagonal belltower with a tent roof and one of the chapels, also with a tent roof, give the church an impressive monumentality and dignity.

A characteristic feature of the churches of this period is that their external appearance often bears no relation to their internal structure. The exterior tends to become a mere superficial decoration applied by the architects to achieve an elegant effect; and the interior is sometimes composed of a number of separate elements which are not combined to form a unified whole.

In the middle of the century the Church began to take exception to this widespread use of decorative ornament as a manifestation of the secularisation of Russian culture. The Patriarch Nikon, that great protagonist of the policy of the Church, whose aim was to establish the pre-eminence of the ecclesiastical over the secular power, laid down his own architectural canons. Religious architecture must demonstrate by its magnificence and monumentality, and by its grandiose scale, the strength and authority of the Church. The large monasteries built by Nikon – the Monastery of the Cross, the Iberian Monastery and the Monastery of the New Jerusalem – were designed to exemplify these new requirements. The cathedral in the Monastery of the New Jerusalem, with its huge tent roof and rotunda, was a building of particular magnificence. It was not possible, however, to turn back the course of architectural development, and even the Monastery of the New Jerusalem showed clear evidence of the quest for decorative effect, which was enhanced by the lavish use of coloured tiles and the disposition of the subsidiary elements built on to the main structure.

The buildings of the mid 17th century began to show a clearer and more logical arrangement of the separate parts, though without abandoning the lavish decoration which had become general. The interiors of the churches were as richly decorated as ever, resplendent with their brightly coloured mural paintings, the rich gilding and carving of the iconostases, and the silver and gilt frames of the icons.

The architecture of the last quarter of the century was of particular individuality, in the characteristic style known as "Moscow baroque" or the "Naryskhin style", after the family of that name on whose estates the most striking examples of the style were built. The churches of this period now showed a more logical sense of layout: the main structure of the building was clearly defined, the central part of the church being given a distinct vertical emphasis, while the subsidiary elements lost their earlier independence and were related to the main structure.

The interiors of these churches are remarkable for their richly carved iconostases, which surpass anything previously achieved in this field. The most striking features of these churches, however, are their exteriors, with their dynamic lines, their abundance of relief ornament, and the intricacy and elaboration of their carving. The "wondrous ornament" for which they were famed, the liveliness of the modelling and the use of white stone are the distinguishing features of this style. Other important elements are the polychrome decoration and the glazed tiles with which the external walls were decorated *(Plate p. 151, below left)*.

A striking example of this style is provided by the Church of the Protection of the Virgin at Fili (1693-94). The octagons of decreasing size superimposed on one another to form the tower, the flights of steps which flank the main structure, and the profusion of decoration combine to create an impression of lightness and grace. The church fits beautifully into its surroundings, and the elegance of the detailing and contrasting pattern of colour show a high degree of architectural refinement which demonstrates the builders' ability to preserve and develop the native traditions of Russian architecture.

In spite of the large numbers of stone buildings in the towns of the 17th century the bulk of the building in towns − and of course even more so in the country − continued to be in timber. Wood was the cheapest and most readily available material, easy to work and familiar through many centuries of use; and the people of Russia were reluctant to abandon the material they loved so well. The buildings erected in this period are unsurpassed for their impeccable sense of proportion, their delicacy of finish and their profusion of carved ornament.

Their builders understood the "soul" of the wood, the beauty and variety of its structure, its colouring, and the characteristics of the different timbers. They were able not only to plan the structure of a building and achieve an exact interpretation of its function, but also to endow it with outstanding aesthetic qualities.

Russian timber churches are light and graceful, usually small but sometimes of considerable size, and almost always of high artistic quality. The soaring upward movement of their bell-towers, the graceful domes surmounted by crosses, and the design and decoration of the windows and doors bear witness to a profound and subtle sense of plastic beauty. How striking, too, is the festive grace of the iconostases, with their profusion of carved ornament, combining vegetable motifs, twisted columns and openwork tracery into a complex decorative pattern! The icons and the scenes from the Scriptures emerge with increased elegance and effect from this riot of painted and gilded carving. Even in the very smallest churches the iconostases are authentic works of art. In other types of building, too, we find wood used with great effect — in town mansions built by skilled craftsmen and in peasants' huts, which were frequently also decorated with carved ornament. And these are traditions which are still alive in our own day.

The houses built in towns were frequently of two or three stories, with a high roof and projecting porches decorated with carving. A striking example of this type of building was the famous royal palace in the village of Kolomenskoe near Moscow, built between 1667 and 1681. This consisted of seven separate buildings linked by passages into a single whole, each part of the structure — which in places was of three or four stories — having its own roof. The external staircases, the corridors, the galleries and the windows were richly ornamented with carving, giving the whole building a picturesque and decorative effect. The internal walls were covered with ornamental and pictorial painting. The palace, a building unique of its kind, had a life of something like a century before it fell into a state of dilapidation and had to be demolished.

Wooden churches with tent roofs were also built in the 17th century, the high "tent" being erected on a square base. Most of these were in the north of the country: in central Russia the preference was for large stone-built churches, cubic in shape, with either a single dome or five domes above a hipped roof.

A new form of architecture now developed to meet the need for commercial and industrial buildings. In Archangel, for example, Dmitry Startsev built a huge complex of commercial buildings, the Gostinny Dvor (Bazaar, Market), with a total length of something like a quarter of a mile, protected by a stone wall with square towers at intervals. Commercial buildings of a new type were also erected in Moscow and other towns.

An example of the large-scale development of stone building in the 17th century is provided by the ancient city of Novgorod, where a new Voivode's Palace in stone was built in replacement of an earlier timber structure. The Palace consisted of a whole complex of buildings, including the Voivode's Residence, churches, towers and ancillary buildings.

The work was carried out on instructions from Moscow that "in future the building should be stout and strong, so that boyars and voivodes might dwell in their residences of stone without constraint or difficulty". The whole palace complex and certain other buildings in Novgorod were erected by an architect sent from Moscow, Efimov.

The process of town development in the 17th century can be followed in the Kremlin of Rostov (1670-83) *(Plates pp. 152 above 156)*, which provides a striking demonstration of the progress made in the art of town planning and of the high degree of skill achieved by the builders of the period. The old Cathedral of the Dormition was left outside the walls, and the new buildings were laid out round a grand courtyard and garden in the centre of the Kremlin. The principal building in the Kremlin was the audience chamber, the White Hall. It is significant that the new Kremlin was not merely an austere defensive structure, as its predecessor had been, but resembled an elegant mansion picturesquely situated on the banks of Lake Nero.

Typical specimens of the civil architecture of this period are provided by the monastery buildings, and particularly by the refectories. As an example we may take the refectory of the Monastery of the

Trinity and St Sergius *(Plates pp. 161, 163)*. This huge vaulted room still makes a powerful impression with its size and spaciousness. Its most striking feature, however, is the design of the external walls, which are remarkable for their sense of proportion and the richness of their architectural detail. This gives the whole building an unusual elegance, and its beauty and impressiveness are increased by the columns which frame the windows, the frieze of scallop-shell mouldings, and the general richness of colouring. The refectory of the Simonov Monastery (1677-80) is another typical building of this period.

Within our own day Moscow has enormously increased in size. New streets and parks have been laid out and new residential areas have grown up, so that the whole face of the old city has been transformed. Many of the older buildings have either disappeared altogether or been reconstructed. Fortunately, however, the mass of new building has not entirely obliterated the fascinating remains of the past, which have survived to provide a lasting reminder of the achievement and the distinctive characteristics of Russian art. The picturesque old churches of Moscow, its stonebuilt mansions, its defensive walls and towers give the city its particular colouring and its special charm, recalling the history of Russia's ancient capital and the glorious traditions of its art and architecture. The 17th century thus played a large part in the creation of the distinctive atmosphere of Moscow as we know it today.

In this period great changes took place in the general pattern and layout of the city. The monasteries were rebuilt, the old winding lanes were replaced by straight streets, timber building was forbidden in the central area, and the new churches which were now erected were designed to fit into their particular place in the plan of their district and of the city as a whole. There was a considerable development of building in stone, not only for churches but also for dwelling houses and public buildings. We know from foreigners who visited Moscow in the 17th century of the magnificence of the city's architecture. "We marvelled at their beauty," writes one of these visitors, Paul of Aleppo; "at the ornament, the solidity, the fine architecture and the elegance of the buildings, their great number of windows and of columns with carved decoration, and the abundance of painting in many colours, both within and without: indeed it seemed that the buildings were in truth decorated with pieces of many-coloured marble and delicately formed mosaics." This statement by a foreign observer provides convincing evidence that Moscow was a town of outstanding beauty and magnificence, a large and populous city which made an overwhelming impression on any visitor.

The town residences of the boyars and merchants had a characteristic layout of their own, usually consisting of an enclosed area within which were a grand courtyard and the mansion itself, often comprising two separate parts joined by a passage. Behind this were domestic offices, a garden and a kitchen-garden. The properties of the richer citizens might include a private church. The whole complex formed an independent unit which nevertheless fitted into the general pattern of the town: indeed these mansions, standing by themselves in a mantle of greenery, added their own distinctive touch of picturesqueness to the urban scene.

The most important group of buildings in Moscow was in its splendid Kremlin *(Plate p. 152 below)*. With the Kremlin were associated all the most important events in the history of Russia, all the most glorious pages of its past. It was the very heart of the Russian state, the incarnation of its power and authority. And in the striking and distinctive beauty of the Kremlin, the buildings within its walls, and the treasures which it contains, we can sense the spiritual greatness and the artistic gifts of the men who created them.

The history of the Kremlin goes back to times of remote antiquity. It was already established as the centre of Moscow by the middle of the 12th century, and the 14th century saw the building of the stone Cathedrals of the Archangel Michael and the Dormition, together with the stone walls and towers of its ramparts. After the famous Battle of Kulikovo in 1380, when the Tatar hordes were routed and Moscow became the capital of the Russian state, the Kremlin underwent an intensive process of rebuilding. For this purpose some of the leading Italian architects of the day were called in − men like Aristotele Fioravanti, Marco Ruffo, Pietro Solari and Alevisio the Second. The Kremlin was enlarged, its walls and towers were strengthened, the cathedrals were reconstructed and the Palace of Facets was built. At this period, too, the tall watch-tower known as Ivan the Great's Bell-tower was built (completed in 1600).

The Kremlin suffered grievously during the troubled period at the beginning of the 17th century. Many of the buildings fell into a state of dilapidation, or were destroyed or burned down. After the Time of Troubles the country began to recover, and considerable building operations were undertaken : the stone palaces of the Tsars, the *Terems*, were built, and the defensive towers were reconstructed *(Plate p. 151 below right)*. It was in this period that the Kremlin took on the appearance which is familiar today.

Even after the capital of the country was transferred to the banks of the Neva in the 18th century building continued in the Kremlin, and the churches and the ancient walls, hallowed by the heroic memories of the past, retained all their significance for the people of Russia.

The walls and towers of the Kremlin as we know them today were the result of a rebuilding between 1485 and 1495 which provided the citadel of Moscow with powerful defences against any attacker; but the buildings within the walls were by no means confined to those associated with the Kremlin's defensive function. The walls of the Kremlin are 20 feet thick and stand over 60 feet high; they have a total circuit of over 2400 yards, punctuated by twenty towers which enhance the beauty and impressiveness of the whole complex. The 70 acres enclosed within the walls contain a great variety of historic buildings, both palaces and churches, making the Kremlin a veritable museum of Russian culture.

The many-storied Borovitsky Tower, built in 1490 by Pietro Antonio Solari, was given a high tent roof in the 17th century. The wall above the River Moskva was reinforced by the building of the Blagoveshchensky, Taynitsky, Petrovsky and other towers; and the severe Beklemishevsky Tower at the south-east corner, built by Marco Ruffo in 1487, was heightened.

The finest of the towers is the Spassky, built by Solari in 1491, which combines monumentality and elegance, severity of line and graceful openwork detailing. In 1625 Bazhen Ogurtsov and the English clockmaker Christopher Galloway added a tent roof and a clock. The niches in the upper part of the tower at one time contained pieces of sculpture, but these were later destroyed.

The 17th century made fundamental changes in the architecture of the towers. The increase in their height completely altered their character, and the soaring tent roofs gave them a distinctively Russian appearance. It is now difficult to imagine the Kremlin towers without their spires, which give the squat defensive architecture of the original towers an air of triumphant elegance.

The architecture of the 17th century was a confident and vigorous art. In spite of its rather limited thematic range it was a clear affirmation of its creators' striving for beauty and perfection. As it developed it extended its range, facing and solving many complex problems of planning and design, achieving its own form of synthesis with painting and sculpture, and grappling successfully with structural problems of great complexity. A significant feature of Russian architecture was its intimate contact with folk art, which gave it a flavour and picturesqueness of its own and enabled it to express the joyous assertion of human values which is so strikingly displayed in many aspects of Russian art in the 17th century.

The painting of the 17th century, a compound of many different elements, has still been very inadequately studied, having — as sometimes happens in the world of scholarship — been neglected in favour of other fields of more immediate interest. The result is that many aspects of the remarkable heritage left to us by the 17th century have not received the attention they deserve and are still an unknown quantity. The circumstances in which many fine pieces of painting were executed remain obscure, and the names of the artists who painted some of the magnificent icons of the period are still unknown. In spite of these deficiencies, however, the significance of the 17th century in the history of painting is now generally recognised; the achievements of the Russian artists of this period are now appreciated at their true worth, and we are accordingly able to assess the importance of their work, and in particular of their painting, in the historical development of Russian art as a whole.

Seventeenth century painting shows evidence of the changes whick took place in the outlook of the artists, of their search for new means of expression, of their departure from the older traditions. It demonstrates clearly the characteristic features of this period of transition between the Middle Ages and modern times. The representation of the real world and of real people now became the principal theme of art. The new interest in nature, in portraiture and in the representation of scenes from everyday life is evidence of a fresh artistic trend — a trend which of course reflected a change in circumstances and in human attitudes.

In this period the asceticism of the Middle Ages was faced with a decisive challenge; and the intensity of the conflict is shown clearly by the controversy to which it gave rise in the field of aesthetics.

The process which began in the 17th century was continued and largely completed in the following century; and the art of the 18th century is thus the result of a rich and complex earlier development.

In the painting of the 17th century we can readily discern two trends which determine its character and give the period its own particular individuality. On the one hand there was a quest for new forms, untrammelled by the dogmatic traditions of the past, secular in character and closer to real life; on the other there was a tendency to maintain established conventions, to erect the traditions of the past into a dogma, to declare their absolute validity and to defend them against the malign influences of the contemporary world. These two conflicting tendencies in art and literature were the determining factors in the evolution of Russian culture during this period. On occasion the conflict developed into an acute controversy, a collision between differing aesthetic attitudes, and sometimes indeed extended beyond the province of art to take on overtones of social conflict.

A new artistic school now developed in protest against the age-old traditionalism and abstractness of religious painting. An important part in the development of the new trend was played by the influence of western European art, with its realism, its closer reflection of everyday reality.

The leaders of this new school were the icon-painter Simon Ushakov, one of the leading Russian artists of the century, and Iosif Vladimirov, who campaigned vigorously for a fundamental change in artistic principles and practice.

A document of outstanding importance in the aesthetic controversy was Vladimirov's famous *Treatise on Icon-painting*, which gave unequivocal expression to the new principles and the new function which art was to serve, and set out the distinctive aesthetic creed of the period. The *Treatise* reflects the clash between different views on the nature and objectives of art which was then engaging the minds of artists. Vladimirov attacks the ignorant icon-painters who "do not understand what is bad and what is good: they hold to ideas that are out of date and attribute a special virtue to those things that have long since fallen into decline and decay." Vladimirov also takes his stand against obsolete traditions, against outdated symbolism, against the conventionalised schematism of the older school of art, against anything that ran counter to the new ideas of the time. It is significant, however, that in relation to western European art and its achievements Vladimirov and other 17th century artists were very far from being mere imitators and by no means set up the art of the West as a model to be copied. What was at issue was the secular content of art, and above all the trend towards realism which appealed so strongly to the foremost Russian artists of the day. The features in foreign art which interested Vladimirov were not only the realistic treatment of religious subjects but the use of purely secular themes — the portraits of ordinary human beings and the artists' ability to "represent all manner of objects and events in their pictures, depicting them as they are in real life." We can see this trend at work in the genre scenes so characteristic of Russian art, of which the Yaroslavl paintings provide some striking examples, on themes taken from everyday life.

Vladimirov inveighs against the commercially produced icons of inferior quality which circulated in large numbers in the remotest parts of the country, constituting "a profanation and a mockery" of true art. The central problem with which he is concerned, however, is the artist's relationship to the subjects he represents. He attacks the adherents of the old conventional style of icon-painting. "Where did these senseless lovers of tradition discover the injunction to paint the figures of saints in this unchanging fashion, always with dark and swarthy faces?" he asks. His *Treatise* was a call to abandon

the conventionality of the traditional style and be guided by reality and commonsense. The effect of flatness which the older style demanded, the conventional attitudes and colouring, the use of allegorical symbolism – all the accepted features which represented a departure from reality were subjected to criticism and called in question. The theme which runs through the whole of Vladimirov's *Treatise* is the demand for naturalism in the representation of the human figure. Painting must seek to reproduce all the light and shade of reality rather than to achieve an artificial flatness and uniformity. In similar vein Simon Ushakov, in his *Word to the Lover of Icon-painting*, exalts the art of painting by comparing it with a mirror which must faithfully reflect the appearance of the external world.

Not unnaturally these new aesthetic ideas encountered fierce opposition from the supporters of the older ways. The principal advocate of the immutability of the church tradition in the field of art was the Archpriest Avvakum. The controversy became involved with the wider question of the relationship between Church and State — the increase of secular authority on the one hand and the Church's strenuous endeavour to maintain its privileges and its influence on the other. And the difficulties were aggravated at this period by the schism within the Church, associated as it was with the social unrests of the day.

Great changes were now taking place in the cultural life of Russia. An interest in secular education was spreading ever more widely throughout the population, particularly among the nobles and townsfolk. Many people in Moscow were becoming increasingly interested in Western culture and science, and increasingly critical of the backwardness of Russian life and of the conservatism which set so much store by outdated traditions. Literature now began to show an active concern with secular themes and increasingly lost its theological character. An interest in the details of everyday life and the personalities of real people is found side by side with accounts of the lives of saints, and some memoirs of the period are remarkable for their colourful language and exactness of observation. We can observe the same process at work in the figurative arts. Nevertheless we may still note a certain reserve in this respect, and sometimes even an indication of contradictory tendencies. Even the most prominent artists of the period could not afford to commit themselves wholeheartedly to these revolutionary changes, and even while making a fundamental break with tradition felt bound to follow it in certain respects. But the admission of themes reflecting the pulsating life of the everyday world into the established compositional stereotypes of painting was the first stage in the collapse of the mediaeval aesthetic system.

The changes which took place in painting during the 17th century showed themselves in a slackening of the hold exercised by symbolism, a preference for narrative subjects, an increasing tendency for pictures to tell a story. No doubt all these new ideas were still on a fairly modest scale, and were not by any means to be found in every field of art; but it was the emergence of these trends which gave the period its distinctive character.

In the first half of the century icon-painting was still in many respects under the influence of the older traditions. This was a consequence of the very nature of the genre and the part it played in the life of the period. Nevertheless the striking feature of 17th century icon-painting is its increasing concern with the phenomena of everyday life. At first this process develops cautiously, as we can see from the icon of "The Council of St John the Baptist" (1629, Tretyakov Gallery) or the "Trinity" (Tretyakov Gallery), in which the traditionalism of the composition and the treatment of the figures are strongly reminiscent of the work of earlier periods.

The new spirit is unmistakable, however, in the icon of the "Virgin of Bogolyubovo" (Tretyakov Gallery), painted in the first half of the century. The figures of the Tsarevich Dmitry and the saints with hands extended in prayer who are standing in front of the Virgin, their faces set in grief and an appeal for help, achieve a genuine expressiveness.

An important contribution was made to the art of icon-painting in the first quarter of the 17th century by the "Stroganov school", so called after the wealthy family of merchants and industrialists whose icon-painting workshops produced icons of a very distinctive type.

The Stroganov icons are notable for exquisite refinement of draughtsmanship, painting technique and composition. Clearly they were intended for private use rather than public display. Small in size, and each devoted to a particular religious theme, they depict delicately drawn little figures with elongated bodies and tiny heads. The attitudes are elegant and indeed rather mannered, and the placing of the figures is designed for ornamental effect. The same themes are frequently repeated. Looking at these icons, we are often reminded of miniatures.

The characters in the Stroganov icons are clad in elegant and brightly coloured garments. They move lightly and gracefully, seeming barely to touch the ground, and are often depicted against a background of tree-covered hills. The painters used a delicately drawn line and a light wash of colour to suggest the elegance and refinement of the figures. The colour scheme is based on the use of pinkish and greyish-green tones with touches of red and with gold lettering. The style shows extreme meticulousness, reminiscent of the delicacy of the jeweller's craft.

The icons of the Stroganov school are usually on narrative themes and are full of details from secular life. As examples of the style we may take such magnificent icons as "The Miracle of St Theodore Tiro" (Russian Museum) and certain works by the leading representative of the school, Prokopy Chirin, such as his "St Nikita the Warrior" (Tretyakov Gallery) and "St John the Warrior" (Russian Museum). These works show all the most characteristic features of the delicate and individual Stroganov style.

It is worth remarking that we can get a direct impression of this style from the work of the craftsmen of Palekh, who have preserved the traditions of the Stroganov school into our own day.

The influence of the Stroganov school was still powerfully felt throughout the first half of the century, as is shown by the exquisite refinement of finish and miniature-like painting technique found in many icons of this period. As an example of this we may take an icon of the "Metropolitan Aleksey" (1640s, Tretyakov Gallery), the composition and technique of which are very reminiscent of the Stroganov school. In the icons produced in Moscow in this period, however, the influence of the Stroganov school gradually declines and gives place to a style of greater austerity; the meticulous finish disappears, the figures become simpler and less consciously elegant. This style is exemplified in the iconostasis of the Church of the Laying On of the Veil in the Kremlin, which shows extreme coldness and fussiness in the treatment of the figures, in spite of the expressiveness of the new manner.

In the middle of the 17th century the main icon-painting centre in Russia was the Armoury in Moscow, where artists not only from Moscow but from other Russian towns were actively at work. The city thus became an important centre of painting, bringing together the finest artists of the day, Individual icon-painters now tended to work within very specialised fields, so that a number of artists were sometimes engaged on a single icon. In the middle of the century the Armoury was also a centre for other types of painters, whose work was in continually increasing demand. It was not, however, in any sense an association of independent artists: the painters were members of a highly organised corporation, with the same status and the same living and working conditions as other craftsmen. The Armoury was also in effect a large art school in which many gifted artists received their professional training.

There were significant variations in 17th century attitudes to icons. Those who were still attached to the older ideas regarded them purely as cult objects and objected to any departure from the accepted symbolism and the traditional patterns, while the more progressive elements in society, including in particular the artists of the new school, sought to establish the icon as a work of art, a reflection of reality, an object of aesthetic value in its own right. This led to a clash of opposing views, and to an outburst of violent controversy and mutual recrimination. The characters depicted in icons must not resemble ordinary people, and the world they represented must not be a mere copy of the everyday world: this was the view of the Church, which was now opposed by the newer and more progressive school of aesthetic thought. The "senseless lovers of tradition" were faced with a new conception of the icon as a work of art. In an epistle addressed by Vladimirov to Simon Ushakov we find these solemn words: "Truth does not follow behind ignorant custom: ignorant custom must give way to truth." Ushakov gathered round him a group of like-minded artists − Zinovyev, Maksimov, Ulanov and Filantyev − whose work reflected a constant quest for new directions in painting.

Of particular interest in this connection is the work of Tikhon Filantyev, which can be judged from his icon of "St John the Forerunner" (1689, Tretyakov Gallery). The principal figure in this icon conveys a sense of genuine sorrow and is painted as a three-dimensional figure of flesh and blood in the new spirit characteristic of the 17th century.

These reforming trends were found not only in Ushakov and his immediate associates. Many artists with the same urge to depart from the accepted mediaeval stereotypes and introduce some vitality into their figures were at work in other towns, beyond the reach of his influence. This new movement, this urge to breathe life into the abstractions sanctified by tradition, was clearly in accordance with the spirit of the age. Among the other artists who showed the same tendencies were Nikita Pavlovets, the painter of a "Trinity" (Russian Museum) and a "Mother of God" (Tretyakov Gallery), and Fëdor

Zubov, who produced icons and paintings containing large numbers of figures which reveal the artist's acute observation of everyday life.

In the second half of the century we find icons representing the lives of saints, round the edges of which are small panels on religious themes, depicted with a lively sense of reality. The vigorous and expressive figures in these icons show a genuine sensibility, a striving to achieve a faithful rendering of the passions, the joys and the sufferings which make up human life.

The icons of Yaroslavl, which show the influence of mural painting, are of particular interest. They represent a wide range of incidents from the lives of saints, in which genre scenes and situations taken from real life are constantly recurring. The close connection between icon-painting and monumental painting can be seen from the icon of "The Miracle of the Icon of the Virgin of Fëdorovo" (Russian Museum), in which some of the scenes show figures engaged in the vigorous activity characteristic of mural paintings. In these Yaroslavl icons the principal figure is usually in the centre of the painting, with a variety of subsidiary scenes depicted behind him on a much smaller scale.

The icons of this period also show an interest in secular themes and in battle scenes representing real historical events. This interest is demonstrated in an icon of St Sergius of Radonezh, dating from the 1650s or 1660s, which contains a frieze representing the Battle of Kulikovo, full of lively incidents from the legend *(Plate p. 190 below)*. The clash of mounted warriors and the hand-to-hand melee are depicted with great vigour and circumstantial detail, as if designed to appeal to an interested and knowledgeable audience.

Monumental painting was perhaps even more strongly affected by the new ideas. The artist's interest in the workaday world and in his natural surroundings found readier expression in this type of painting than in the icons. This can be seen, for example, in the frescoes in the Princess's Monastery in Vladimir, in the paintings in the Moscow cathedrals, and elsewhere. Although maintaining the accepted compositional patterns, the artists enriched their design with themes taken from real life. The colour schemes of the mural paintings also underwent a change : even in the first half of the century bright greens, blues and pinks are found, greatly enhancing the liveliness and brilliance of the painting. In the first half of the century much painting was done in the churches of Moscow. A typical example was the painting of the Cathedral of the Dormition in the Kremlin (1642-43), where the work was carried out under the direction of Ivan Paisein, Sidor Osipov, Mark Matveev and others. The composition of these paintings was entirely traditional − figures of the "Saviour not Made with Hands", "Lord of Hosts" and "The Almighty" in the domes, angels on the vaulting, and apostles, prophets, saintly warriors and church festivals on the piers. Unfortunately not all the painting of this period has survived, and much of it was restored at a considerably later period; but the 17th century work that has come down to us shows the sense of innovation and the elegance which is found in so much of the painting of this period.

The largest enterprise of the 1650s and 1660s was the decoration of the Archangel Cathedral in the Kremlin, the burial-place of the Tsars and Princes of Russia. The artists engaged on this work included Yakov Kazanets, Iosif Vladimirov, Simon Ushakov and Gury Nikitin. The paintings are mainly devoted to the Archangel Michael *(Plate pp. 174, 175)*, the patron saint of the Princes of Russia, but also include figures of the Princes and Tsars themselves. They are dedicated to the glorification of the secular authority of the State in all its manifestations. Other typical examples of the work of the period were the frescoes in the Church of the Trinity at Nikitniki (Moscow), reproducing subjects taken from western European engravings — a new development in monumental painting. These subjects were considerably modified and given an entirely new significance; but the very fact that they were used at all is of interest.

Religious themes were now less prominent in the paintings than in an earlier period, their place being taken by subjects of secular concern and by an interest in terrestrial reality and ordinary life. The religious myth frequently took on the form of a historical tale, sometimes based on real life, sometimes frankly fabulous. The new themes were often used in the galleries and porches of churches, but increasingly played a part in the decoration of the churches themselves.

Moscow continued to be the main centre of monumental painting, but this type of painting flourished also in Yaroslavl, Vologda and Kostroma. The Yaroslavl paintings are masterpieces of 17th century art, with a vivid colouring and lively narrative quality which puts them in a class by themselves. The interiors of the Yaroslavl churches were overlaid with a rich pattern of decoration made up of the most variegated motifs, in a style which was quite new in Russian monumental painting. The walls were covered with small pictures, arranged in separate bands or registers, mostly showing scenes from ordinary life, which were often linked in a consecutive sequence. In these pictures stories from the Old and New Testaments were presented with great liveliness and in a simple and straightforward way — often in the form of a series of incidents from everiday life — so that their message was conveyed at once to the spectator.

The most typical example of a Yaroslavl church decorated in the new style is the Church of the Prophet Elijah (1680) *(Plates pp. 176, 190 above)*. The paintings were the work of a team of artists under the leadership of Gury Nikitin and Sila Savin, who had previously worked in Moscow, Rostov and other towns.

The upper part of the church is decorated with frescoes on entirely traditional themes, but the five bands of painting in the lower part contain a well-known series of narrative scenes in which the religious subject matter becomes of secondary importance compared with the lively and entertaining representation of incidents from real life. In depicting the story of Adam and Eve and their expulsion from Paradise' for example, the artists set their characters in a background which has clearly been taken from life, and are concerned to achieve an accurate representation of the natural surroundings, of real animals and birds, and of architectural details.

The most interesting series of paintings is the cycle devoted to the lives of the prophets Elijah and Elisha, containing a sequence of vividly depicted scenes in which stormy seas alternate with peaceful rural landscapes, the prophets rub shoulders with ordinary country folk, and representations of miracles are found side by side with scenes from everyday life. As an example we may take the magnificent fresco showing Elisha restoring the Shunammite's son to life, in which the main action becomes secondary to the picture of a harvesting scene. We see the reapers gathering the rye, clad in blue and pink garments and wielding sickles. Their attitudes and movements, the yellow corn and the trees in the background build up a picture which is clearly painted from life. It was only in the 17th century that a subject of this kind, treated with such remarkable realism, could have found its way on to the walls of a church. And indeed scenes from everyday life are of frequent occurrence in 17th century painting. The Church of the Prophet Elijah, for example, also contains pictures of ploughing, house-building, and many similar subjects. The frescoes in this church are also notable for the beauty and elegance of the principal figures and the important part played by ornament, which is woven into the very fabric of the narrative.

No less typical of the period is the Church of St John the Forerunner in Tolchkovo (1695), which was decorated by a group of artists under the leadership of Dmitry Plekhanov. Notwithstanding the austerity of the subject matter and its treatment in comparison with the paintings in the Church of the Prophet Elijah, these paintings too are striking examples of the new style, the artists' new relationship to their subject matter and their lively imagination. In the scenes representing the chastisement of sinners the artists achieve a powerful effect and a strikingly lifelike rendering of the figures. The pictures of the woman who has murdered her child, the Boat of the Godless and the expulsion of sinners are of great dramatic force, and the representations of the Last Judgment, crowded with figures of devils and monsters, the flames of Hell and the wretched sinners, reflect all the luxuriance of the folk imagination.

The bright pink and blue tones of the Yaroslavl frescoes created a variegated decorative pattern of extreme elegance which enhanced the richness and splendour of the churches. The paintings depicted real characters, often clad in the ordinary garments of the day as worn by peasants or boyars; but the artists also showed an interest in distant and exotic lands which was expressed in a variety of fantastic representations. Some of the paintings were on fabulous themes, appealing to men's imagination and their urge to comprehend the vastness and variety of the world. On the other hand the Yaroslavl frescoes tended to lack the severe monumentality which had been characteristic of the mural painting of the previous century. This is seen particularly in a failure to subordinate the painting to the architectural pattern of the interior; frequently, indeed, the painting bore no relationship to the architecture and became a mere decorative overlay. The pictures themselves, however, gave expression to themes of universal interest, and the composition as a whole was so striking and impressive that they achieved a powerful effect. They depicted a complex and many-sided world, a world which sometimes seemed remote from the observer but gradually developed into a clearly realised picture of reality. In this respect the paintings were very characteristic of their century, exemplifying the distinctive features of its artistic philosophy.

With their optimism, their feeling for reality and their profound novelty, the Yaroslavl frescoes inevitably influenced the work of other artists. In consequence we find a certain similarity between the Yaroslavl painting and the decoration of churches in other towns, an identity of artistic approach and a community of style. Typical examples of the painting of the period are found, for instance, in churches at Borisoglebsk — e.g., the frescoes in the Romanov Cathedral — and at Suzdal and Vologda. These show the same narrative manner and the same interest in secular themes as we find at Yaroslavl.

The notable feature of 17th century monumental painting is the dynamic force of the composition. In their striving to paint as complete a picture as possible of all the manifold activities of human life, the artists not only unfolded their narrative in a series of separate scenes, each one leading on to the next, but also — in striking contrast to the painting of earlier centuries — liked to represent their figures in violent movement, in bold foreshortening, in constant restless activity.

It remains true, however, that although the artists' eagerness to depict scenes from everyday life and to tell a story reflected their desire to apprehend as fully as possible the world which surrounded them, their treatment of the human figure was still in many respects traditional. It was still beyond their power to portray man's inner nature, his mind and spirit and character. This was to be the achievement of a later period in the history of Russian art.

The most important artist of the second half of the 17th century was Simon Ushakov (1626-86), a craftsman of outstanding professional skill who enjoyed great reputation and authority, and whose works give us the fullest expression of the characteristic features of the period. In addition to his creative work he is known as a theoretical writer. Standing as he did above the narrower interests of different groups and schools, he can be regarded as the leader of the artistic movement of the century.

Of his origin nothing is known. After many years of productive work in the Armoury he was raised to the ranks of the nobility, an honour only rarely accorded to artists. He was skilled in a wide range of crafts — drawing, engraving, icon-painting and monumental painting — and was in charge of the execution of the most important paintings of the period, in the Cathedral of the Dormition and the Archangel Cathedral in the Kremlin.

One of Ushakov's most popular icons is his "Saviour not Made with Hands" (1657, Tretyakov Gallery), a representation of Christ's head on the Vernicle. The subject was a common theme of icon-painting, but in Ushakov's hands it received a new interpretation. The novelty of the work lies in the method of treating Christ's face, in a markedly three-dimensional form which distinguishes it from other treatments of the same theme. The face is drawn with extreme restraint, with no effort to achieve expressiveness and no sense of inner movement; but in painting it the artist was clearly seeking to achieve the same realism as was appropriate in the portrayal of an ordinary human being.

We find the same qualities in Ushakov's icon of the "Trinity". While preserving the traditional structural pattern, he shows himself an innovator in the field of artistic form, achieving a most lifelike and down-to-earth effect in the representation of his figures. Other characteristic icons by Ushakov are his "Archangel Michael" and his "Mother of God" (both in the Tretyakov Gallery). The distinctive feature of Ushakov's "Trinity", and also of his icon "The Lord's Supper", is his attempt to obtain a lifelike effect by the use of linear perspective, thus breaking away from the long established tradition of representation in a single plane and at the same time bringing out the concrete reality of the event depicted.

It must be admitted that Ushakov's "Trinity" lacks the harmony and profound philosophical significance of Andrey Rublёv's icon on the same subject. The attempt to achieve vivid realism in the representation of the scene has to some extent overshadowed the revelation of the deeper recesses of she human mind and spirit. Moreover the weakness of Ushakov's work lay in the poverty and monotony of its colouring.

The saints depicted·in Ushakov's icons are immeasurably nearer ordinary human beings than those in earlier icons. Their faces are painted in bright colours, the volumes are conveyed by the use of light and shade, and the hair is rendered with a smooth wash. The figures are remarkable for their naturalness: a characteristic which was entirely new and represented a daring and stimulating departure from the conventional style imposed by tradition. As an example of Ushakov's work, and one which illustrates the originality of his approach, we may take "The Tree of the Russian Kingdom" (Tretyakov Gallery), an allegorical composition representing the establishment of the kingdom by Ivan Kalita and the Metropolitan Peter, who are shown planting a tree which stands for Russia. The representations of the Kremlin and the Cathedral of the Dormition, and even more strikingly the portraits of Tsar Aleksey Mikhaylovich and Tsarina Mariya, show a powerful sense of realism. In this work exact portraiture was combined with allegorical significance, which itself had a precise historical reference and was immediately comprehensible to the observer. This concern with portraiture was characteristic of all Ushakov's work; and we know from the written sources that he painted portraits on canvas of Tsars Aleksey Mikhaylovich and Fёdor Alekseevich.

In his engraving of "The Seven Deadly Sins" Uskakov shows great skill in depicting the various attitudes and expressions of the naked human body. There are a number of other engravings based on drawings by him.

The 17th century saw the development of a new genre of painting in Russia, the *parsuna* (from the Latin *persona*) or representation of an ordinary human being. This was not yet a portrait in the modern sense — the *parsuna* lay somewhere between a realistic portrait and an icon — but it was an original and distinctive work of art in its own right. There was an active school of *parsuna*-painting not only in Russia but in the Ukraine.

The icon-painters now developed a characteristic manner in which, while many of the techniques of icon-painting were preserved, the figures were no longer abstract but wholly concrete, representing distinctive personalities and real human beings. As a rule the *parsuna* was painted on a wooden panel, though examples on canvas are also found. The artist's technique was almost exactly the same as with an icon. He hollowed out a cavity on the surface of the panel, the "shrine", covered this with a ground coat, sketched out his design and then laid on the colours. These works preserved not only the formal

characteristics of icon-painting but the same artistic vision, the same conceptions of perspective, of space and of colouring. The figures were rigid, represented in a single plane, with no facial expression. The artists showed great interest in the representation of ornament, and frequently also in the inscriptions giving the names of the characters or other explanatory material.

But although the techniques used were those of icon-painting the figures represented were no longer abstract personages but real living people. The artists aimed at a faithful rendering of their distinctive individual characteristics, and the shapes of the heads, the faces, the figures and the garments were all taken from life. And yet, although the people depicted in these works are recognisable individuals, they are still caught up in the rigidity and conventionality of icon-painting and have not yet come to life.

The *parsuna* had long existed as a genre in Russian art, but the period of its greatest flowering came in the 17th century. Paul of Aleppo, describing the tombs in the Archangel Cathedral in Moscow in 1655, records that "above each tomb is a figure of the occupant as he was in life." Vladimirov also speaks in his *Treatise* of the necessity of achieving a faithful representation of the human figure in the *parsuna*, and many of the artists of this period painted from life. The interest shown in the *parsuna* was in fact merely one aspect of the contemporary concern with human personality.

In our eyes the *parsuna* has many archaic features, but to the men of that day it was a new form of art, an entirely novel type of artistic creation which was closely related to everyday life and reality.

Outstanding examples of the 17th century *parsuna* are the portraits of Tsar Aleksey Mikhaylovich Romanov, shown holding the orb and sceptre of royalty, and his son Tsar Fëdor Alekseevich (both in the Historical Museum in Moscow). Another characteristic example which illustrates all the distinctive features of the genre is a portrait of Prince M.V. Skopin-Shuysky (Tretyakov Gallery) *(Plate p. 185)*, a prominent 17th century statesman and a successful military commander who freed many Russian towns from foreign occupation and later died by poison, administered by his enemies. His dark green kaftan is covered with gold and silver brocade and richly adorned with pearls and precious stones. The round face, the high forehead, the bold upward curve of the eyebrows and the small round eyes make this the portrait of a distinctive and recognisable individual. At the top of the picture are an inscription and a representation of the "Saviour not Made with Hands". The rigidity of pose and the manner of rendering the ornament are still very characteristic of the icon-painting tradition; but at the same time we are struck by the genuine individuality shown in the portrayal of the sitter.

Another typical *parsuna* is a large canvas by an unknown artist representing the nobleman V.F. Lyutkin (1698, Historical Museum). This is not merely a small head-and-shoulders figure, but a large-scale formal portrait. Lyutkin is shown at full length and in life size, against the background of a red velvet curtain. Here again, however, the figure is represented in a single plane and in accordance with the accepted conventions; and − again following the traditions of icon-painting − there is no sense of space.

It was this genre, however, which gave rise to the realistic portrait, later to play such a prominent part in the history of Russian art. The *parsuna* represented a transitional stage between the icon and the portrait, which was by no means an 18th century invention but had a considerable pedigree of its own.

The graphic art of the 17th century shows many new features. It was a period of intensive development of the various genres, and of a steady increase in significance. Like 17th century painting, the graphic art of the period showed a constant interest in new methods and new ideas.

The records have preserved the names of a large number of engravers and draughtsmen who worked in the Pechatny Dvor, the Moscow printing-house, during this period, including such leading artists of the day as Ushakov, Zubov and Chirin.

In the first half of the century the art of the woodcut rose to importance. It was practised both in Moscow and in other towns, particularly in monasteries, and was used to illustrate books of both religious and secular character. Particularly fine examples of the graphic art of this period are the woodcuts by Kondraty Ivanov in a *Gospel* published in 1627, which is remarkable not only for its fine portraits of the Evangelists but for the beautifully executed decorations in which each page is framed. Of great interest also are the woodcuts in an *Alphabet* of 1637, which illustrate the text with a variety of scenes from everyday life, including a number of genre subjects.

In these works we are struck by the artists' skill in tracing their delicate patterns on wood, by the virtuosity with which they are able to render ornamental scrollwork, architectural detail and the human figure. In later years the traditions of wood-engraving were to be perpetuated in folk art, in popular prints and broadsheets *(lubki)*.

In the second half of the century the woodcut gave place to the new technique of engraving on metal, which represented an advance in refinement. An early, but already entirely professional, example of engraving on copper is Simon Ushakov's print of "The Seven Deadly Sins", in drypoint technique; and the same artist was responsible for other engravings which appeared in books of the period. Another outstanding master of the art of engraving was Afanasy Trukhmensky, who produced many fine prints.

Seventeenth century engraving is a rich and productive field which has close connections with the work being done in other genres at this time. It has not yet, however, received the thorough study which it undoubtedly requires.

Russian sculpture can look back on a long history, the origins of which are lost in the mists of time; and the early masters of plastic art, like artists working in other genres, created works which expressed the great aesthetic ideals of the period.

Throughout the whole course of its development Russian sculpture was intimately connected with folk art, and this gave it a distinctive national identity and a characteristic beauty of its own.

The works of ancient Russian plastic art which have come down to us attest the considerable development of this genre and the prominent place which sculpture occupied in the life of the people. Many of the works which have survived are reliefs depicting a variety of allegorical scenes, or sometimes merely vegetable or geometric ornament. Of particular quality are the ornamental motifs, which show an exuberant imagination, an interest in decorative patterns and a shrewd appreciation of the possibilities of the medium.

Although the use of sculpture in churches was frowned on by the ecclesiastical authorities, it nevertheless contrived to make a considerable place for itself in the form of reliefs, carved ornament, the framework of iconostases and the *oklady* (masking frames) of the numerous icons. In all this work religious themes alternate with secular subjects, contemporary motifs with old pagan ones, and carving by skilled professional artists with work in the folk tradition, producing a diversity of pattern which gives it an unmistakable identity of its own.

The favourite material of the early Russian sculptors was wood. The passage of time, however, inevitably erodes the substance of the wood, blurs the sharp outlines of the carving, smoothes down the contrasts and destroys the colouring. It is a short-lived material which does not stand up to the ravages of the centuries. Nevertheless the few examples of wood carving that have survived are sufficient to indicate the remarkable beauty and the infinite variety of form which it achieved in its day.

Much of this work was of a religious character, and most of it was intended for the embellishment of churches. In spite of this it was not wholly confined within the requirements of ecclesiastical dogma; for the craftsmen whose carvings decorated the churches of the day were concerned to express their own conception of reality.

The carved decoration of the iconostases of the period — either sculpture in the round or carving in low relief — is remarkable for its elegance, its rich beauty and its exuberant imagination. A riot of carved garlands soars upwards in an intricate and fanciful pattern; the paintings are framed in splendid carved ornament, gilded or painted; and the surface of the iconostasis may be enriched with wooden figures of saints or cupids, adding to the total effect with a rich interplay of light and shade.

This carved ornament was a characteristic and essential element of the iconostases of the period: it was part of the very structure of the iconostasis and not merely a frame for the painting, adding an element of plastic beauty which enhanced the total effect. The decorative possibilities of carving were fully realised, and were exploited with great skill to create elegant church interiors. Although in the early part of the century the decoration of the iconostasis retained the flatness of the previous period, the pattern changed in the second half of the century. The carved decorations became much more three-dimensional and more complex in design; carving in high relief, and sometimes fully in the round, became increasingly common. In some churches, indeed, the icons and the painting are no longer the central feature but take second place to the richly carved ornament of the iconostasis.

As a rule the iconostases were decorated with complex patterns of vegetable ornament — including fruit, elaborate garlands and flowers — which varied widely from church to church. The carving was usually covered with gilding. Through all its diversity of design, however, the ornament of the iconostases had to fit in with certain structural requirements. The vertical colonnettes, which were often twisted, emphasised the soaring upward movement of the screen, and the position of the doors was marked by a semicircular arch.

Good examples of the use of carving to decorate church interiors are provided by the "royal doors" from a church in the village of Vozdvizhenskoe, near Zagorsk, and the Church of St John the Forerunner in Tolchkovo. In these buildings the carving has become an end in itself. Carved ornament of extraordinary richness is also found in the royal doors from the Church of St Nicholas of the Great Cross (now in the refectory church in the Monastery of the Trinity and St Sergius) *(Plate p. 189)*, the iconostasis in the Church of the Dormition in Pokrovka, and the iconostasis in the Church of the Sign in Dubrovitsi.

In the 17th century wood continued to be the sculptor's main material, being used on a large scale not only in churches but in ordinary secular building. The mansions of prosperous citizens were richly decorated with sculpture and with carved surrounds to the doors, windows and balconies. Carving was also much used for interior decoration. According to contemporary accounts the carved ornament of the old timber palace in the village of Kolomenskoe was of particular splendour, being known as "the eighth wonder of the world".

The skill of the carvers was also applied to the decoration of various articles of domestic use. Chairs, tables, cupboard doors and the lids of wooden chests were covered with intricate ornament, often based on vegetable motifs and incorporating birds and animals, all ingeniously combined into an intricate and homogeneous pattern.

The evolution of sculpture in the round during the 17th century shows the same general processes at work as in painting. The representations of Christ and of the saints become much more three-dimensional and realistic and stress the individual characteristics of the figures. Typical examples of this are figures of a hermit (Russian Museum) and St Parasceve or St Pyatnitsa (Perm Museum) *(Plate p. 189)*. Although still maintaining the static pose and the constraint of the traditional style, they are nevertheless remarkable for their realism and human individuality. Wood sculpture was almost always painted in bright colours, giving it an immediate appeal.

In the sculpture of the 17th century we also meet some of the favourite figures of Russian tradition, treated by different artists in their varying ways — in particular St George the Victorious, St Nikita the Warrior and St Nicholas of Mozhaysk.

The Museum in Perm contains a collection of material which is of particular importance to students of the history of sculpture in wood. This shows the usual traditional features, with a distinctive local tinge which enhances their expressiveness and effect.

As a characteristic example of 17th century plastic art we may consider a magnificent figure of the Tsarevich Dmitry on a silver reliquary from the Archangel Cathedral in Moscow, carved in 1630 by Gavrila Ovdokimov *(Plate p. 187)*. The figure of Dmitry is treated three-dimensionally. He is shown against a richly decorated background, wearing a splendid garment adorned with precious stones, the ornament on which combines with the background to form a unified pattern. The expression on the Tsarevich's face, his rather broad cheekbones and his staring eyes are accurately rendered, but at the same time the artist has managed to convey the youthfulness and naturalness of the boy's face. Another work showing similar characteristics is the figure of Aleksandr Svirsky (1643, Russian Museum), which is also carved on the cover of a reliquary.

The sculpture of the 17th century includes many representations of animals and birds, and in particular of lions — the symbol of power — which were used in the most varied decorative contexts. Whether curled up in a ball or stretched out at full length, these lions are always full of expressiveness; often they are distorted with great virtuosity into a geometrical pattern and perform an almost purely ornamental function.

Elements of plastic ornament were also widely used in applied art, on a variety of dishes and vessels, on silver cups and goblets, on articles of church furnishing, and so on.

Thus the sculpture of the 17th century not only developed with remarkable vigour but evolved many characteristics that were entirely new. As in the field of painting, realistic elements became predominant, while sculpture in the round gradually superseded the conventional low relief of earlier years and the representation of the human figure played an increasingly important part.

Applied art also made rapid progress during the 17th century. Although much work of this kind was destroyed or plundered during the Time of Troubles at the beginning of the century, the various crafts developed with renewed vigour in the following period, and the losses of earlier years were largely made good. The goldsmiths' and silversmiths' workshops in Moscow were kept busily employed producing jewellery, for which there was an enormous demand, stimulated by the ostentatious luxury of the court and the feudal nobility.

Much artistic effort was also devoted to the decoration of various articles of domestic use. Dishes, combs, cups and other objects produced by the craftsmen of this period were often real works of art. Bone-carving and glass production also developed on a considerable scale. The chief centre for the production of such objects was again the Kremlin Armoury.

The technique of engraving metal, particularly silver, now came into use. Some cups dating from this period, on which the ornament is usually left bare but the ground is covered with niello, are of striking and individual beauty.

These works of applied art show great variety of technique and design; and work of high quality was produced by various local schools, each with its own distinctive characteristics.

Many works of folk art also have a particular charm. Wooden vessels of various kinds, embroidery, furniture and decorative painting played a considerable part in the life of the 17th century, providing evidence of the lively imagination and the eternal quest for beauty which was so abundantly expressed in the artistic creation of ordinary people.

Equally remarkable are the various articles forged from metal — locks, hinges, doors, objects of everyday use, ornaments. In this period craftsmen did not merely produce articles of this kind for their own use but also manufactured them for sale. The local markets of Russia were now united to form a single market, and this facilitated a wide distribution of the output of local craftsmen.

An important branch of applied art was the production of *oklady* (frames) for icons and liturgical books. The exquisitely delicate ornament, the richness and variety of the relief, and the precious stones with which they were inlaid contributed to make these *oklady* works of the highest artistic quality. The edges of the frames sometimes contained a number of separate panels or medallions depicting a variety of different themes.

At the end of the century the technique of enamelling appeared, and rapidly achieved great popularity.

The many objects of applied art dating from this period which can be seen in the Kremlin Armoury, including some treasures from the collections of Princes and Tsars, make an immediate appeal to the visitor's imagination and convey some impression not only of the prodigal luxury of the Russian court but also of the exquisite skill of Russian craftsmen, their vigorous creative imagination and the remarkable folk traditions to which they gave expression.

The art of the 17th century represents the culmination of the development of the older Russian art. We can see it today as a period of splendid achievement which crowned the history of mediaeval Russian culture. Seventeenth century art did not in any sense mark a decline or an anticlimax: it had great qualities of its own and showed a spirit of innovation which produced a rich harvest of aesthetic achievement.

At the end of the 17th century a great stratum of the native culture of Russia passed into history. The start of the new century was a turning point, a frontier between the old and the new; and there is perhaps no more significant frontier in the whole course of Russian history. But this does not mean that the art of the older Russia disappeared without trace. The traditions of the 17th century proved remarkably persistent and played an important part in the culture of the following period. The new and forward-looking elements in Russian art were cherished and carefully preserved into our own day, while the outdated and reactionary elements were swept away during the turmoil of the 18th century.

VII The Eighteenth Century
a Period of New Discoveries

The 18th century is a period of great significance in Russian history: "an age of intelligence and an age of extravagance", an age of great discoveries, of astonishing scientific advance, of far-reaching transformations in the structure of the Russian state.

During this period Russia developed from a backward country of which western Europe knew little into a rich and powerful nation of steadily increasing authority. It was in this period, too, that the country cast off the fetters of the Middle Ages and the human mind was able to pursue in unrestrained freedom its quest for understanding of the laws which governed the natural world. "Unforgettable century, which to delighted mortals grants truth, freedom and light!" wrote Aleksandr Radishchev. And yet it was also a period of savage repression which saw the triumph of serfdom, the enslavement of the peasants and the reduction of the mass of the people to hopeless pauperism.

The 18th century saw not only a mighty upsurge of the social consciousness of the Russian people and a great advance in social and philosophical thinking, but also a rich flowering of art. The great names of Russian science and literature — Lomonosov, Fonvizin, Radishchev, Derzhavin and Novikov — are matched by those of artists like Shubin and Rokotov, Levitsky and Bazhenov, Kozlovsky and Losenko, whose work gave expression to many of the fundamental ideas of the century and enriched the heritage of Russian culture.

In spite of its long history Russian art was still a young art, engaged in a process of intensive development, advancing to fresh achievement in reaction against older ideas, and eagerly assimilating new ideas which had hitherto been beyond its compass. Its growth during this period was remarkable: new genres were created and developed, new themes were treated, new standards of artistic form were achieved.

This development received a powerful stimulus at the beginning of the century, during the reign of Peter the Great, when Russian art, reacting against the influence of the outmoded mediaeval culture, established itself as a secular and realistic art, fully responsive to the needs of contemporary life. This was not, however, achieved without difficulty, for throughout the century the representatives of the new trend found themselves in perpetual conflict with those who still clung to the older ideas.

In recent years the study of 18th century Russian art has advanced rapidly. The work of the artists of this period has been collected and recorded, carefully studied and restored; and this has greatly enlarged our knowledge of its development and has contributed to the great reputation which it now enjoys.

In spite of the substantial progress which its industry and trade had made in the 17th century Russia was still far behind the more advanced nations of western Europe. The country's greatest handicap was its unnatural isolation, its lack of any access to the sea, which was a major obstacle to the development of trade. Progress could be made only by resolute measures designed to achieve a complete transformation.

Then came the "Northern War" against the Swedes, which lasted twenty-one years but finally ended in victory and in the liberation of Russian territory and the opening up of the Gulf of Finland. Russia had now gained an outlet to the sea and had become a great maritime power.

During Peter's reign Russian industry made rapid progress, a powerful fleet was built and a national army created. Science and learning advanced as never before, the output of the printing presses increased, and the first Russian newspaper appeared. New educational institutions were established and a reform of the administrative machinery carried out, with the creation of the Senate and the twelve administrative "Colleges". Peter made the Church subordinate to the State and established the Synod to manage ecclesiastical affairs. The Petrine period was a time of great changes in Russia — changes in the national way of life, in manners and in dress. It was not surprising, therefore, that Russian art also underwent a change.

Peter the Great's achievement was to deliver Russia from its condition of mediaeval backwardness and make it one of the most powerful nations in Europe. In this process all that was obsolete and outdated was rejected, and the new elements which matched the spirit of the age received the encouragement and support which enabled them to develop. Mediaeval Russia was now finally relegated to limbo. Not unexpectedly, the administrative changes introduced at the beginning of the century encountered many difficulties and much opposition. The result was a bitter conflict in which victory was bound to go to the shrewdest of the contestants, the man who knew his objective and set out boldly to achieve it; and Peter's success in carrying through his plans made him one of the most popular European statesmen of the day.

Unfortunately a number of works published in Europe and America have been concerned to propagate the idea that Russian art in this period was dependent on foreign art, that it lost its national characteristics at the turn of the 17th and 18th centuries. This is not a new theory, but has been current for something over a hundred years. As early as the beginning of the 19th century the Slavophils, in denying the legitimacy and historical appropriateness of the changes carried out by Peter, were led to reject also the new school of art, which they regarded as imitative and alien to the national culture of Russia. This was also the view of some later critics. Towards the end of the 19th century and in the early years of the 20th it was unequivocally expressed by the Russian art historians N. Vrangel and A. Benois. Thus Vrangel refers in one of his works to the "two centuries of confusion and disorder in the cultural life of Russia" which began in the early years of the 18th century. In his view Peter the Great had done Russia a disservice in forcibly injecting alien standards of artistic style, and Russian art was an "artificial amalgam" created by foreigners. The same point of view, expressed in different words, can still be heard in our own day.

Soviet art historians have long since demonstrated the error of such views. A careful study of the material now available has made it possible to reach a clearer understanding of the history of 18th century Russian art; and this has not only enlarged our knowledge of its development but has enabled us to study its relationship with the art of other countries and has illuminated the process of emergence of the new secular and realistic art. The Russian realism of the 18th century was not an importation

from the West, nor the result of imitating Western fashions, but was a natural and profoundly national phenomenon with a long-established and extremely fruitful tradition rooted in the past. Russian realism resembles the corresponding foreign schools in the same way as French art resembles Italian or German ; but these resemblances do not in any way obscure the special characteristics or the distinctive national identity of the different schools.

Those who argue against the independence of Russian art usually make great play with the country's active links with the West in the 18th century and the large number of foreign artists who worked in Russia. These facts are not in dispute, but they by no means lead to the conclusion which is drawn from them.

Peter the Great did in fact offer a ready welcome to foreigners, since he was anxious to benefit from their experience in the various fields of science and culture. The assimilation of this foreign experience was one of the prime objectives of this period, for it would have been folly to leave Russia to pursue a course of slow and gradual evolution, taking no account of the progress already made in the West. At the very beginning of the century several hundred foreign specialists came to Russia; and later, after the introduction of a law giving them special privileges and freedom of worship, their number was substantially increased. Among them were artists like the engraver Adrian Schönebeck and the sculptor Konrad Osner; later came the painters Louis Caravacque, Gottfried Danhauer and Georg Gsell and the sculptor Carlo Rastrelli.

These foreigners came to Russia on contract for three years, and usually then returned to their own country. Some of them, however, stayed in Russia and came to regard it as a second home. The great majority remained faithful to their native style of art and played no part in the development of Russian art. Only one or two of these incomers showed a real awareness of the requirements of Russian society, set themselves new aesthetic objectives, and created works which can properly be considered as belonging to the history of Russian art.

Peter, anxious that his country should profit from the achievements of foreign artists, sent young men into other countries, enjoining them to concern themselves with whatever might be of use to Russia. It is significant that not one of the Russian artists whose stay abroad was financed in this way became a mere mechanical imitator. They learned the secrets of their craft, the principles of realistic draughtsmanship and the laws of anatomy, studied the heritage of the old masters and familiarised themselves with the work of their contemporaries; but all of them preserved their national individuality, so that their work can be distinguished at once from that of a foreign artist. The same method of assistinh young artists to travel abroad was employed in other European countries at this period, with no less fruitful results.

Peter the Great's active concern with the development of art was dictated by his recognition of its vital importance. Thus the circumstances of Russian life in this period favoured the development of book production, and Peter sought to promote this craft by every possible means. "We cannot do without the artist and the engraver," he wrote, recognising the importance of providing illustrations for the literature which was now being published. For this purpose there was associated with the St Petersburg printing-house a special school for the training of artist illustrators. During Peter's reign a project was put forward for the establishment of an Academy of Arts, to provide proper professional training — "without which," the proposal suggested, "artists cannot have a sufficient grounding in their crafts." Unfortunately Peter's untimely death delayed the realisation of this plan by thirty years.

The new ideas of the day were reflected in an impressive flowering of architecture. Never before had there been such intense building activity in Russia as in the early years of the 18th century. The building industry was reorganised to enable it to meet the new demands. New factories were established for the production of building materials, a standard size of brick was introduced, and general directives were issued on the design and construction of buildings. New types of structure appeared for the first time in Russia, in a vast programme of building and civil engineering work which included shipyards, works of fortification, factories, canals and locks, museums, administrative buildings and much else besides.

The new tasks which now faced the architectural profession underlined the need to train architects of wide competence capable of dealing with commissions of considerable scale and complexity. Books were published on the theory of architecture, special schools were established, and students were sent abroad at State expense. The first students sent abroad in this way during Peter's reign were Ivan Korobov, Pëtr Eropkin, Ivan Mordvinov and Ivan Michurin, who were subsequently responsible for much building work and made important contributions to the history of Russian architecture.

The first buildings of the 18th century were erected in Moscow, and showed the features which were to be typical of later Russian architecture. These buildings were the Menshikov Palace (also known as the Lefort Palace), built in 1707-08, and the Arsenal in the Moscow Kremlin (1702-06), with its splendid entrance designed by D. Ivanov and M. Choglokov.

The most important and characteristic building erected in Moscow in the early years of the century was the Menshikov Tower (1704-07), designed by the gifted architect and sculptor Ivan Zarudny. This church, cruciform in plan and richly embellished with carved ornament, was originally crowned with a spire and bore a strong resemblance to the "tent"-roofed churches of the 17th century; it was also the undoubted prototype of the Cathedral of SS. Peter and Paul in St Petersburg. The scrolls on either side of the entrance, the pilasters and the series of superimposed openwork octagons combined to give the building an air of lightness and elegance. Unfortunately a fire in the year 1723 destroyed the graceful spire and radically altered the appearance of the church. Zarudny was responsible for many other buildings in the city, including a triumphal gateway, a hospital, churches and houses. He was the leading Moscow architect of the early part of the century.

The Church of the Virgin of the Sign at Dubrovitsi, one of the masterpieces of Moscow architecture of the end of the 17th century and the early years of the 18th, is also attributed to Zarudny. Its very individual plan, its profusion of carved ornament and its octagonal tower finished with an iron coronet are very reminiscent of the baroque architecture of the architect's native Ukraine.

Thus in the early years of the 18th century there was intense building activity in Moscow, and its architecture, based though it was on the traditions of the previous century, began to develop a style characteristic of the new age. But this was only the beginning of the process : for the fullest and finest development of Petrine architecture we must look to the new capital of Russia, St Petersburg.

The establishment of a new capital city on the banks of the Neva, the transfer of the administrative centre of the country to a situation where it would be nearer the other countries of Europe, was an act of extreme boldness justified by a grandiose conception of policy. The new capital was intended to be an important military, commercial and cultural centre : it was to be Russia's "window on Europe".

The city was founded in May 1703, with the establishment of the fortress to which the name of St Petersburg was given ; and in 1712 it was officially declared the capital of Russia. As the surrounding territory was recovered from the Swedes the city grew enormously and soon developed into a homogeneous community of an entirely new pattern, very different from the older Russian towns. It was laid out on a unified plan, largely determined by the course of the Neva and centred on the fortress. The new capital was built in stone, in sharp contrast to Moscow with its few stone churches lost in a sea of timber houses. Since there was no stone in the St Petersburg area, a decree was issued requiring all who entered the city to bring "three stones in each cart-load" as a contribution to the building of the capital. Soon a special Building Department was established to be responsible for the construction of the city. The streets were laid out on geometrically straight alignments, giving St Petersburg a very different aspect from the older Russian cities founded in the Middle Ages. From the beginning, too, standard house plans were laid down for citizens of different degrees of wealth and social position ; all of them, however, being relatively unpretentious and differing only in size.

As an example of the rationally planned architecture of this period we may take Peter's own Summer Palace, still to be seen in the Summer Garden. It is a relatively small building showing extreme restraint in the use of decoration, somewhat reminiscent of the residences of Dutch burghers. Peter had a particular liking for Dutch architecture, being impressed with its simple and functional style. Moreover the experience of Dutch builders seemed likely to be of particular value to St Petersburg in view of the similarity of the geographical conditions ; for the abundance of water and the marshy ground on the banks of the Neva gave the surroundings of St Petersburg some similarity with the landscape of Holland. The buildings erected in the new capital in the early years of the century, however, had a distinctively Russian character, with only a very remote resemblance to Dutch architecture.

The builders of St Petersburg were faced with some unusually complex problems. The draining of the marshes, the improvement of the river banks, the procurement and transport of timber and stone, and finally the erection of the buildings and the laying out of the streets cost many thousands of human lives. In spite of all difficulties, however, the town was built in a remarkably short space of time and became one of the handsomest cities in the world.

The foundation of St Petersburg provided a powerful stimulus to the development of Russian art, since the city offered hundreds of skilled architects, sculptors, painters and other artists full scope for the exercise of their talents. The first buildings erected in the new capital were the Fortress and the Cathedral of SS. Peter and Paul. These were originally built in timber, but were later reconstructed in stone. They were designed by Domenico Tressini (c. 1670-1734), a native of Italy who settled in Russia and spent thirty years of his life there.

The fortress and the cathedral became the real centre of the city *(Plate p. 204 below right)*. The extensive circuit of walls, with massive bastions projecting towards the river, had a menacing and formidable aspect which bore witness to the might of Russia. The structure of the fortress was remarkable for its homogeneity, and the architecture, while wholly functional, succeeded at the same time in achieving elegance and magnificence. This is particularly well exemplified by the famous Petrovsky Gate (1717-18), also designed by Tressini and decorated with carving by Konrad Osner *(Plate p. 204 above right)*. Its distinctive baroque character is based on a strict conception of architectural function combined with the rational use of plastic ornament. The gate is a feature of notable elegance, while the fortress itself is an austere and ascetic structure ; and it is precisely in this contrast that the architect seeks his effect.

The fortress is dominated by the Cathedral of SS. Peter and Paul, which with its massive tower and tall spire is one of the outstanding landmarks of the city. It is true that the exterior − in a style rather reminiscent of the Menshikov Tower − is not particularly impressive ; the interior, however, is magnificent. The most important feature of the building is the bell-tower, a three-storied structure which is drawn into a unified whole by the volutes on the angles and is crowned by the soaring spire with its figure of an angel. The spire can be seen from a great distance, and adds a distinctive note to the skyline of the city.

The iconostasis in the Cathedral, carved by Ivan Zarudny, is a magnificent and very typical example of Petrine architecture. The richness of the modelling and the profusion of carved figures combine with the painted icons and the brightly coloured paintings under the dome to create an effect of great elegance and splendour. The pictures in the Cathedral were mostly painted by Russian artists.

Tressini's most important work, after the Cathedral of SS. Peter and Paul, was the Twelve Colleges in St Petersburg (now the State University), erected between 1721 and 1733 to house the various administrative departments of government. This was a long range of offices lying at right angles to the Neva, designed as a unified whole but with the separate sections distinguished by individual façades with pilasters and a small pediment, and with independent roofs. During the early years of the century, too, building was carried out along the Neva embankments. Near the Twelve Colleges was built the Kunstkammer designed by Georg Johann Mattarnovi and Mikhail Zemtsov, with a characteristic octagonal tower linking the two lateral wings of the building. On the same embankment, a little downstream, was the Menshikov Palace designed by G.M. Fontana and Gottfried Schädel, a small building with projecting wings and pavilions, decorated with pilasters and a small semicircular pediment. As was normal with buildings along the river front, there was a small landing-stage in front of the palace, and behind it were various appurtenances, including a pleasure-garden, a kitchengarden and domestic offices.

During the 1720s and 1730s the architects principally engaged in the building of St Petersburg were Korobov, Zemtsov and Eropkin. Zemtsov was responsible for laying out the Summer Garden and for building the "Halls of Ceremony" in the Garden, as well as for designing St Isaac's Church and the Anichkov Palace. Eropkin's name is associated with large-scale town development operations in St Petersburg.

Meanwhile the Admiralty dockyard was built on the left bank of the Neva and became the central point of an important district of the new city. From this point radiated three main thoroughfares: the Nevsky Prospekt — the principal street of the city — Gorokhovy Street and Voznesensky Street. The building of these streets substantially enlarged the scale of the city. At first the Admiralty had all the appearance of a fortress. It was surrounded on three sides by ramparts and a moat, and the angles facing on to the Neva were reinforced by bastions from which cannon could command the river. Even in later years, when the danger of attack had disappeared, the building did not lose its fortress-like appearance, retaining its defences until the early years of the 19th century.

The Admiralty buildings were laid out in the form of the Greek letter π, with the open end facing the Neva, and consisted of a long range of two-storey buildings containing workshops, stores, armouries, foundries and so on. Considerable changes were made in the 1730s, when the building was reconstructed to the plans of Ivan Korobov. At this stage the Admiralty acquired its famous tower with the spire crowned by a ship, forming a focal point at which the principal streets of the city met *(Plate 204, above right)*.

The Admiralty remained in this form throughout the 18th century, and it was not until 1805 that Adrian Zakharov undertook a large-scale reconstruction of the building. At this period it took on more or less its present appearance *(Plate p. 204 above left)*. The original Petrine building with the characteristic high roof and the modest pilasters ornamenting the façade was transformed into a classical structure with four pillared porticoes and a profusion of sculpture and carving. The ramparts and bastions were swept away and the moat was replaced by a treelined avenue, so that the building was now thrown open to the citizens of St Petersburg. It had in fact long ceased to be a dockyard, and now housed the administrative headquarters of the Russian navy. Fortunately Zakharov appreciated the merit of Korobov's spire and preserved it in its entirety, merely framing it in a classical colonnade.

The buildings erected in St Petersburg in the early years of the century differ in many respects from the architecture of 17th century Moscow, but they also show traditional features. One obvious example of this is the Cathedral of SS. Peter and Paul, which has no parallels in western European architecture but shows close links with earlier Russian building.

From the early years of the 18th century the development of the city proceeded on an organised plan. Great stress was laid on the regular design of the façades, the decoration of which had to be fitted into the framework of the classical orders. The buildings were embellished with volutes, figured pediments and carving, but this decoration was kept within reasonable bounds: the ornament was always restrained so that it played its proper part in the total architectural effect.

The building activity of Peter's reign was not of course confined to Moscow and St Petersburg. Much building was also done in the provinces. At Taganrog, in the Urals and Altay, at Tula and Petrozavodsk, and at Kazan there were erected individual buildings and large architectural ensembles showing in greater or lesser degree the characteristics of the Petrine style, its soberly functional approach, its restrained decoration and its logical organisation of structure. Among the many magnificent parks and gardens which were laid out during the 18th century Peterhof (now called Petrodvorets), on the shores of the Gulf of Finland near Leningrad, is outstanding for its beauty and the plastic unity of its design. It was created in the early years of the century as the summer residence of Peter the Great, and from the outset amazed foreign visitors by its magnificence, which entirely belied the accepted ideas about the backwardness of Russia.

The park and the Great Palace, built in the baroque style by Bartolemmeo Rastrelli, lay on higher ground, with cascades and fountains decorated with sculpture running down the slopes. In the lower park, which stretched down to the shores of the Gulf of Finland, were other fountains and pavilions *(Plates pp. 202 above, 202 below, 203)*. Of particular interest is Peter's private palace of Monplaisir, a single-storey building with large windows and a high roof in the Dutch style. Here Peter lived, dealt with government business and received foreign envoys. From the palace there was a view of Kronstadt, the principal fortress in the Gulf of Finland and the key to St Petersburg. Peterhof was designed by Peter himself. His original drawings have been preserved, showing the main buildings and fountains. The most impressive part of the whole complex is, of course, the Great Palace and its cascade, from which a canal runs down to the Gulf, flanked by two lines of small fountains *(Plate p. 202 below)*.

With their powerful upward-soaring jets and their variety of design the fountains of Peterhof achieve a gay and striking effect. Their chief interest lies in their sculpture. Originally this was in lead, but at the end of the 18th century the earlier work was replaced by bronze statues by the Russian sculptors Prokofyev, Shchedrin, Shubin and Martos. The central feature was a figure of Samson rending open the lion's jaws — an allegory of the battle of Poltava, in which Russia had decisively defeated the Swedes. This group, by Mikhail Kozlovsky, was rightly considered a masterpiece of decorative sculpture. Seen through the spray of the fountains, with the sunlight glittering on the water, these gilded figures take on a special beauty of their own.

Peterhof was frequently the scene of elaborate court festivities, in the preparation of which many skilled artists were employed. Of particular splendour were the firework displays, which were mounted with great lavishness and made a powerful impression on all who saw them. An English visitor wrote that anyone wishing to describe them must "dip his pen in a sea of rainbow-coloured ink."

Side by side with the construction of houses and public buildings and the laying out of parks, the old religious architecture in timber continued to develop during the early years of the 18th century. Of the considerable number of such buildings erected in this period perhaps the most fabulously beautiful as well as the most strikingly individual was the Church of the Transfiguration at Kizhi on Lake Onega, built in 1714 *(Plates pp. 210, 211)*. This is a remarkable demonstration of the virtuosity and individuality of Russian architects, their soaring imagination and magnificent technical mastery. The church, built on the very shores of the lake, standing 120 feet high and embellished with twenty-two domes, makes an unforgettable impression on the visitor. A variety of legends and traditions grew up round this building, which was reputed far and wide as a marvel of architectural skill; and it is easy to see why.

The timber domes are arranged in a pyramidal pattern, in a soaring upward movement which gives the church its special beauty and picturesqueness. The uniqueness of its proportions and silhouette, the masterly organisation of volumes and the delicacy of the carving combine to demonstrate the superb skill of the builders. The church was constructed without a single nail; and it is said that when the architect, Master Nester, had completed his task he flung his axe into the waters of the lake, with the words: "There has never been, is not, and never shall be such another!" And we are compelled to admit the truth of this claim.

The period of Peter the Great was notable for its concern with human personality, its belief in the limitless possibilities open to man; and this eager interest in man produced a vigorous and fruitful development of portrait-painting, as well as influencing the whole course of development of Russian art.

A factor of fundamental importance in this connection was the great interest taken in Russia from the beginning of the 18th century onwards in the study of the physical world. This interest was a very characteristic feature of the period. Russian science made great strides, an Academy of Science was founded, new schools were established, book production expanded. The study of nature and the effort to understand the inner meaning of the processes which men saw at work in the world around them were foremost among the preoccupations of the age; and this inevitably had its effect on the art of the period and promoted the development of the principles of realism.

The art of icon-painting, governed by mediaeval conceptions of human life and the function of art, was no longer adequate in the 18th century to express the strivings of the new age and give substance to the contemporary aesthetic ideal. The realities of life, in all their variety and infinite complexity, presented the artist with new problems and required new forms and techniques for their expression. The artists of the 18th century had not merely to learn to draw and paint in a different way, but to see and interpret differently a whole world of real and not merely abstract values. On the other hand the older ideas which had grown up in the course of the centuries had become part of the very substance of art, had acquired an immensely rich tradition, and were taken for granted through sheer force of habit. It was inevitable, therefore, that the development of the new secular and realistic art should give rise to the bitterest controversy.

Icon painting did not die out in the 18th century. Considerable numbers of icons were painted in this period, many churches were decorated with painting, and the traditions of the genre were preserved. But inevitably the new secular and realistic art had an effect on the character of religious painting, influencing both its subject matter and its artistic form.

The characteristics of the new style were shown most clearly in the field of portrait painting. From the early years of the century we have the series of portraits of the "Unholy Synod" – the name Peter jokingly gave to the boon companions of his leisure hours, in ironical allusion to the Holy

Synod which governed the Church. These portraits bear all the marks of a period of transition. They are still strongly imbued with the influence of the *parsuna,* although in many respects they show similarities with the realistic portrait which was to become so popular in the 18th century. The figures are still represented in a single plane, although the individual likeness of the sitter is now much more clearly expressed than in the *parsuna.* The artist still tends to include the traditional ornament, and sometimes there is an inscription attached to the portrait. Typical examples are the portraits of Vasikov, Count Apraksin and Yakov Turgenev *(Plate p. 228).* The best of the series is the portrait of Turgenev, whose face is presented with great realism, though the pose still shows a certain rigidity.

This series of portraits is of great importance as an illustration of the direction in which painting was developing at the turn of the century, and can be seen as occupying a transitional position in the history of secular and realistic art.

The leading practitioners of the new style in the first part of the 18th century were Andrey Matveev (1710-39) and Ivan Nikitin (c. 1690-1741). Matveev was a scion of a noble family who found his way to St Petersburg as a young man. There his enthusiasm for painting brought him to Peter's notice, and his future career was decided. He was sent to Holland, where he spent some years perfecting his skill. Thereafter he returned to Russia and devoted himself to decorative painting, being responsible for the decoration of numerous buildings in St Petersburg, including in particular the Cathedral of SS. Peter and Paul. He also achieved fame as an unusually gifted portrait painter, a characteristic example of his work being his "Self-portrait with Wife".

Ivan Nikitin, the son of a Moscow priest, had a very different career, and one which ended in tragedy. In his youth, while a singer in a court choir, he also worked as a portrait painter, in which field he showed remarkable talent. Thereafter he spent some years in France and Italy. Even before going abroad Nikitin was well known to the Tsar, who was always ready to help and encourage any artists who showed particular gifts. Peter took pride in Nikitin's skill, and when the artist visited Danzig asked his wife Catherine, who was staying there at the time, to use her influence to secure him a commission for a portrait of the Polish king Augustus II − "so that it may be known," wrote Peter, "that we too have skilled craftsmen".

Returning to Russia in 1718, Nikitin acquired a considerable reputation and painted a long series of portraits of his contemporaries.

Nikitin's work has broken free from the influence of the *parsuna* and is remarkable for its fine draughtsmanship and accurate likenesses, as well as for its penetrating insight into the character of the sitter. As an example of these qualities we may take his portrait of Peter the Great (Russian Museum) *(Plate p. 226).* Peter's portrait was painted by many artists, both Russian and foreign, who were usually interested in the figure of the Emperor, the man who ruled over the destinies of a great Empire, the great military commander. He was therefore frequently represented wearing armour and a military cloak, or sometimes on horseback, clad in magnificent garments, against the background of a battle. The distinctive quality of Nikitin's portrait, on the other hand, is it profound humanity. Although the picture shows only Peter's head it conveys a powerful impression of his intelligence and humanity. Nikitin sees Peter as a thinking, suffering man, and this is what distinguishes his work from many other contemporary portraits of the Tsar.

226

ѦКОВЪ : ТѶРГЄНЄКЪ :

Nikitin also painted a well-known portrait of "Peter the Great on his Deathbed" (also in the Russian Museum).

A painting which is generally regarded as one of his best works is his "Portrait of a Hetman" *(Plate p. 227)*, evidently painted in the middle 1720s. This is a striking likeness of an elderly warrior who gazes sternly at the spectator, his furrowed brow and intent stare reflecting the hardships he has endured in the course of his service. It is a portrait of great psychological penetration which reveals the inmost being of the sitter.

The process of breaking free from the traditions of the past was inevitably accompanied by difficulties and conflicts, and in effect occupied the whole of the 18th century. The persistence with which some artists still clung to the old tradition of the *parsuna* is demonstrated in the work of Ivan Nikitin's brother Roman, who was still firmly attached to the traditional style. In spite of his obvious talent and technical proficiency he was still dominated by the ideas of the older school. This can be clearly seen in his portraits of members of the Stroganov family *(Plate p. 225)*. With their rigidity of pose, their schematic draughtsmanship and their delight in ornament, these works seem extraordinarily old-fashioned in comparison with the profoundly realistic portraits painted by Ivan Nikitin.

After Peter's death there were many changes in Russia; and there were changes also in Ivan Nikitin's life. He was accused of opposition to the government, arrested, flogged, and sent to Siberia. Some years later he was pardoned; but the hardships he had undergone had sapped his strength and he died on the way back to St Petersburg.

The construction of the new capital gave a stimulus to the development of decorative painting, which was much in demand for the embellishment of the new palaces and public buildings. The novel features of this genre were its secular subject matter and its extensive use of allegorical themes, which were depicted with great concreteness and often reflected real historical events. Unfortunately little of the decorative painting of this period has been preserved, since most of the buildings have been destroyed; but we can gain an impression of its quality from the paintings in the palace of Monplaisir at Peterhof, in the Summer Palace and in the Kadriorg Palace in Tallinn.

The new pattern of life in Russia was reflected also in graphic art, which from the earliest years of the 18th century was in process of active development. Indeed it was perhaps this branch of art which first showed the effect of the new trends which were appearing in Russian culture. It developed in two directions — easel drawing and illustration. (We have already referred to Peter the Great's interest in the development of book production, which was closely bound up with the work of the engravers).

In the early days it was found necessary to reinforce the native Russian artists by bringing in a number of foreigners, the most important of whom were Adrian Schönebeck and Peter Pickaerdt. The former did not stay long in Russia, but Pickaerdt remained for over ten years.

An outstanding contribution to the art of engraving in Russia was made by Aleksey Zubov (1682 to after 1744), an artist trained in the Moscow Armoury, who produced a famous series of views of

St Petersburg. These prints give us a faithful picture of the new capital, with its palaces, its wide avenues and parks, its network of canals and the bustling life of its streets. Apart from their purely documentary value Zubov's prints are highly competent works of considerable artistic merit.

Later, in the 1750s, a further series of engravings of St Petersburg was produced by another prominent artist engraver, Mikhail Makhaev (1716-70). In contrast to Zubov's disciplined draughtsmanship, his work was smoother and more picturesque, and he was more catholic in his choice of subjects than the artists of the early years of the century. He did not confine himself exclusively to the city of St Petersburg, but portrayed scenes in the suburban districts and in palaces and parks, as well as in Moscow.

In the early years of the 18th century there was also a remarkable growth of interest in sculpture. It is generally considered that the most flourishing branches of art in this period were architecture, graphic art and portrait painting; but sculpture by no means fell behind these other genres. The creation of the new capital, the erection of numerous palaces and public buildings, the laying out of parks and the interior decoration of the new houses all led to a demand for works of plastic art. It was at this period that the special qualities of sculpture and the great possibilities of the medium first began to be fully realised.

The early years of the century saw an increased interest in classical sculpture and an appreciation of the high degree of professional skill which it had achieved. Significantly, it was during these years that the splendid ancient marble figure of the Tauride Venus was acquired in Italy and brought to St Petersburg. It was installed in a specially constructed pavilion in the Summer Garden, and is now one of the treasures of the Hermitage. The developing interest in sculpture naturally turned men's thoughts towards Italy, both ancient and modern; and it was accordingly to Leghorn that a group of gifted young artists were sent to be trained in the art of sculpture.

The great importance of sculpture in the life of Russian society is demonstrated by the extensive use made of it in the decoration of Peterhof. Sculpture was also the principal form of decoration in the Summer Garden and the source of its exquisite beauty; and it similarly contributed to the charm of many other parks in and around St Petersburg, Moscow and other towns.

Sculpture was also used with great skill for the adornment of the new buildings erected in the cities of Russia. The rational simplicity of early 18th century architecture was enriched with plastic decoration, principally in the form of simple reliefs and mouldings, which harmonised perfectly with the clear-cut outlines of the façades, the curved volutes of the cornices and the capitals of the pilasters. In this period the whole aspect of the city, the lines of the façades and the pattern of streets and squares were conceived in plastic terms.

The wooden carving found in so many churches in northern Russia — including not only low relief but sculpture in the round — remained within the folk tradition. The works of these local craftsmen, who are for the most part nameless, are remarkable for their acute observation and perfection of skill.

The collections of this sculpture in the museums of Vologda and Perm contain work of outstanding merit which has not yet been the subject of detailed study. These local sculptors have something of the monumental style of the icon-painters, combined with an acutely realistic vision of the world. And many other museums in Russia also contain examples of wood sculpture which are notable for delicacy and individuality of conception and masterly skill in the use of polychrome painting *(Plate p. 221)*.

The foreign sculptors who came to Russia in the early years of the century — Nicolas Pineau, Andreas Schlüter, Konrad Osner and others — made relatively little contribution to the development of Russian plastic art. The only one of them to achieve a position of any prominence in the history of Russian sculpture was Carlo Rastrelli (1675-1754), who found in Russia a second home and wide scope for the employment of his gifts. He was a prolific worker in the most varied genres, but it was in the field of portrait sculpture that he showed the full measure of his talent. An outstanding example of his work is his famous bust of Peter the Great, an entirely convincing presentation of the dynamic figure of the Emperor. Designed for effect but yet profoundly true to life, filled with the fierce energy and resolution of the sitter, this work represented an entirely new achievement in portrait sculpture. Other important works by Rastrelli which have survived are a bust of Prince A. Menshikov, a statue of the Empress Anna, a self-portrait and some decorative sculpture. Although not remarkable for psychological insight or delicacy of modelling, Rastrelli's works were valued for their undoubted professionalism, a quality which Russian sculpture was still striving to attain.

Rastrelli's name is linked with the history of two major monuments which were conceived in the early years of the century. The first of these is the so-called "Triumphal Pillar", a work dating from Peter's reign on which Rastrelli was engaged along with Andrey Nartov and Nicolas Pineau. This was to be a tall column entirely covered with reliefs representing incidents from the Northern War, the foundation of St Petersburg and other events. Unfortunately a variety of circumstances prevented the execution of this project, and the column exists only in the form of a model; but even this conveys a clear impression of the outstanding qualities of the design.

Rastrelli's other large monumental work, which he was able to bring almost to completion, was an equestrian statue of Peter the Great. A large model of the monument was completed before the sculptor's death; but although the statue was cast in bronze it was not erected and was lost to sight for many years. Then, in the 1760s, when it was again proposed to erect a monument to Peter the Great, it was decided not to use Rastrelli's work. In the second half of the century Peter was thought of mainly as a wise statesman and legislator, the man who had transformed and modernised Russia; and accordingly Rastrelli's horseman was not thought appropriate to the occasion. Thereafter the statue was again forgotten until the very end of the century, when its existence was remembered almost by accident; and in 1800, on the directions of the Emperor Paul I, it was at last erected in front of the Engineers' Castle (formerly the Michael Castle).

The achievement of Russian art in the early 18th century were made possible by the cultural development of the previous century. The rich traditions inherited from the past continued to develop in the new conditions, preserving the essential homogeneity of Russian art and giving it a marked national individuality.

The Mid Eighteenth Century

The period after Peter the Great's death was a difficult one for Russia. A struggle for power began, one court faction ousted another, foreigners gained increased influence, and the headlong tempo of the early years of the century gave place to a more moderate pace. The substitution of one ruler for another, however, could not hold up the historical process. The country went through a particularly difficult time during the reign of the Empress Anna, when the prodigal luxury of court life was in glaring contrast with the poverty of the ordinary people and the Empress's foreign favourites rose to unprecedented influence, so that in effect it was they who governed the country. A reflection of this period can be seen in Carlo Rastrelli's sculptured group "The Empress Anna" *(Plate p. 248)* – in the sombre grandeur of the conception, the splendour of the Empress's elaborate dress, well expressing the character of the "Empress with the fearful glance", as she was called. A degree of stability was achieved only with the accession of Peter's daughter Elizabeth in 1741.

In the history of Russian art the post-Petrine period is sometimes considered an age of decline. This is a misconception. Art continued to develop, and nothing could halt its advance. No doubt there was a slackening of pace, but that was all. During this period a number of great decorative painters and portraitists were at work, and architecture continued to progress.

The middle of the 18th century was a period of great achievement in Russian architecture. There was much building of palaces and large churches, and the baroque style came to full flowering. Luxurious palaces, lavishly decorated with carving and painting, and splendid parks were created to meet the needs of the Imperial court and the great feudal magnates; but in this period much less effort went into the erection of public buildings.

In the buildings of this period the decorative sculpture formed an important part of the total architectural effect and was conceived as an integral part of the whole. Architects made extensive use of architectural details — pilasters, half columns, columns and round pediments — to create an impression of splendour and magnificence. The decorative effect of mid 18th century architecture was still further enhanced by the use of colour to set off the purely plastic qualities of the structure.

In this period, too, were created the great parks at Kuskovo near Moscow, Tsarskoe Selo near St Petersburg, and elsewhere, which demonstrated the pre-eminent skill of Russian landscape gardeners.

An outstanding architect who left his distinctive mark on the architecture of the period was Bartolommeo Rastrelli (1700-71), son of the sculptor. In this earliest buildings he still showed restraint in the use of decorative elements, introducing pilasters and occasionally vertical ribs of rusticated stone but only rarely employing sculptured ornament. Already, however, he had developed the conception of a building designed for purposes of display, in which he was later to demonstrate his matchless skill. Typical examples of his work are the Vorontsov Palace (Leningrad) and the reconstruction of the Great Palace at Peterhof. In the interior of the palace at Peterhof, with its profusion of carved ornament, the wealth of applied decoration created the effect of magnificence and graceful elegance which is characteristic of Rastrelli's style. This building was already the work of a mature artist with a fully developed mastery of technique and a considered view of the function of architecture.

In the later 1740s Rastrelli's work showed the full measure of its achievement. To this period belong his best known buildings — the Winter Palace, the Catherine Palace at Pushkin (formerly Tsarskoe Selo) and the Smolny Convent in St Petersburg.

In the Catherine Palace *(Plate p. 224 above left und right)* Rastrelli was faced with the task of incorporating various structures belonging to the old palace in a new building of tremendous size, in such a way as to achieve a homogeneous style and an impression of magnificence. Suites of reception rooms, conceived as a unified whole, lead to the Throne Room, and this sequence of rooms constitutes the principal feature of the palace. The elegant doors with their elaborate decorative mouldings, the ceilings with their riot of carved and gilded ornament, and the exquisite parquet flooring combine to create an effect of elegant splendour; and the exterior, with its colour wash of white and blue, its gilding and its Atlas figures, is no less impressive.

The Winter Palace *(Plate p. 233 above)* is another building of great magnificence. It consists of a square range of buildings surrounding a grand courtyard, with extensions at the four corners. The columns on the external walls and the carved decoration of the cornices are very characteristic of Rastrelli's style and enhance the effect of richness and splendour. The interior was designed in the same baroque style, but a century later, in 1837, it suffered serious damage in a fire and was reconstructed. Standing as it does at the very centre of the city, the Winter Palace is an impressive demonstration of the high level of achievement attained by Russian architecture in the 18th century.

Finally we have another magnificent example of Rastrelli's skill in the Smolny Convent *(Plate p. 234 right)*. He was unable to finish the building, though we can judge the quality of his design from the model which has been preserved; but even in its present form Smolny is a building of remarkable originality and talent. The cathedral in particular achieves an admirable unity between the masses of the interior and the articulation of the exterior. The lavish ornament was designed to make the building stand out against its surroundings, and the bell-tower to give it the necessary magnificence. The whole building is remarkable for its lightness, its soaring upward movement, and its relationship with its environment – all achieved by a carefully considered distribution of volumes.

In addition to his work in St Petersburg Rastrelli did much building in other cities – in Moscow, Kiev and the Baltic area. An outstanding example of his work is the Cathedral of St Andrew in Kiev, which has become an integral part of the city pattern and contributes a distinctive feature to its skyline.

Other architects were also active at this period, producing a large number of notable buildings. Among them was Savva Chevakinsky (1713 to after 1783), who designed the Naval Cathedral of St Nicholas in St Petersburg *(Plates pp. 234 above left, 234 below left, 235 right)*. Basically cruciform in plan, this five-domed church stands in a large square and is one of the finest buildings in the city. It is notable for its large carved iconostasis, which lends a unique beauty to the interior.

Leading Moscow architects of this period were Ivan Michurin (1703-63), who made lavish use of decoration in his buildings, and his pupil Dmitry Ukhtomsky (1719-75). Ukhtomsky continued the construction of the famous bell-tower of the Monastery of the Trinity and St Sergius (Zagorsk), which was begun by Michurin *(Plate p. 235 left)*. Starting with a massive foundation structure, he erected on this a series of four stories of progressively diminishing size, pierced with arches and with columns at the angles : a design which gave the tower the elegance and the soaring upward movement characteristic of baroque architecture. With its beauty of proportion and graceful design the bell-tower is one of the finest achievements of mid 18th century Russian architecture. Ukhtomsky occupies an important place in the history of Russian architecture as a great teacher, the founder of an architectural training school which produced many distinguished architects, including Vasily Bazhenov, Matvey Kazakov and Aleksandr Kokorinov.

Among other architects who were active in the middle of the century were Andrey Kvasov, who designed a large cathedral in Kozelets (Ukraine), and Fëdor Argunov, who built the Sheremetev Palace in St Petersburg and a country residence for the same family at Kuskovo on the outskirts of Moscow.

The complex of buildings and parks at Kuskovo is a typical example of the type of suburban establishment favoured by the nobility in this period *(Plates pp. 236 below, 241 below right)*. Kuskovo is a rare example of a successful synthesis between architecture and the countryside, between painting and sculpture, which has preserved all the atmosphere and flavour of the 18th century. The palace itself is typical of the architecture of the period, with its reception rooms arranged *en suite* and its lavish use of sculpture and painting for decorative purposes. The whole place is a museum full of valuable works of art. The palace is not, however, an isolated element in the over-all design, but stands in an organic relationship with the park, the lake, the avenues of trees and the shrubbery. The decorative sculpture in the park, the vases and the ornamental railings give Kuskovo its particular charm and its special flavour of the past. Work on the palace and the park continued throughout the 18th century, but the bulk of the building was completed between the 1750s and the 1770s.

Another outstanding example of the same style is the palace of Ostankino on the outskirts of Moscow *(Plates pp. 243, 244 above)*.

The middle of the 18th century saw a particular flowering of decorative sculpture, which was widely used in many baroque palaces and public buildings which are remarkable for their magnificence of proportions and luxuriance of ornament. Perhaps at no other period in the history of Russian architecture was such lavish use made of plastic ornament in architecture. The work of Bartolommeo Rastrelli is a perpetual demonstration of the use of sculpture for the internal and external decoration of buildings. In the Catherine Palace at Pushkin sculptured detail sometimes takes the place of architectural detail as a means of creating a particular decorative and plastic emphasis at the most important points in the design. The massive Atlas figures on the ground floor form a strong three-dimensional element to which the whole plastic pattern of the façade seems to be related. Along with the more restrained design of the first floor and the mouldings of the cornices and pediments, this profusion of plastic ornament creates an effect of elegance and gaiety. With all its exuberance, however, the sculptured decoration of Russian baroque buildings never obscures the rythm or functional quality of the structure. There is a similar profusion of sculpture in the interior of the building. Intricate mouldings provide a frame of exquisite elegance for the panels of painted decorations. Here again the sculpture, without losing its own independence, plays an important part in bringing out the full significance of the architectural conception.

The baroque style is mainly based on the exploitation of plastic form, with its dynamism, its cascade of three-dimensional masses and its dramatic interplay of light and shade. It is a world of restless movement in which only the functional requirements of the architecture restrain the unending flow of sculptural form and give it the necessary logical pattern.

A leading figure in the world of painting in the middle of the century was Ivan Vishnyakov (1699-1761), an accomplished decorative artist and portrait painter. As a decorative painter he took part in the decoration of many buildings in St Petersburg and the surrounding area; as a portraitist he is particularly known for his portraits of William and Sarah Fermor (Russian Museum).

His portrait of Sarah Fermor (c. 1750) *(Plate p. 259)* is one of his most delightful works. At first glance there seems to be nothing new about the composition of the picture: a column, a vista of landscape, a canopy, providing a background for the standing figure of a girl — elements which are common enough in portraits of this period. The representation of the figure, however, is a work of exquisite skill. Sarah Fermor, wearing the splendid dress of a lady of fashion, complete with wig and fan, is full of vivid reality and poetic truth. Her wide eyes gaze demurely out of the picture. The consciously elegant position of her arms and the rather constrained pose do not detract from the naturalness of the portrait. In spite of the formal setting the personality of this young girl, scarcely more than a child, emerges clearly from the picture. Vishnyakov has caught all the charm of youth and embodied it with great delicacy in his portrait.

It is characteristic of the period that the portrait still retains something of the style of the *parsuna* – a rigidity of pose, a certain flatness of form, a concern with the rendering of ornament. The flowers on Sarah Fermor's dress are scattered over the surface of the material with little regard for three-dimensional form, in the manner familiar to us from the *parsuna*. This mingling of old and new, however, merely enhances the charm of the work. The artist's skill is also shown in the use of colour, based on a subtle interplay of tones of pearly white. Vishnyakov was a painter of great individuality and technical mastery whose work has not yet been adequately studied; but there can be no doubt of his standing as an artist and as a representative of his period.

The work of Vishnyakov and his contemporaries shows that the traditions of the *parsuna* in portrait painting had not been completely displaced in the earlier part of the century. These traditions proved extraordinarily tenacious, continuing for many years to exist and to exert influence on artists. It is sometimes suggested that the pattern of Russian art was set by these traditional features, which maintained its link with icon-painting and the conventional style of the *parsuna*. This is, however, an erroneous view. In the early years of the century Russian painting had turned away from the conventionality of religious art and entered a new channel of development. Artists were now faced with fresh tasks, and the essential qualities of their work are to be seen not in the elements of artificiality which they inherited from the past but in their much more subtle revelation of character and in their entirely secular conception and realistic expression of human personality.

As another example of this we may consider one of Vishnyakov's contemporaries, Aleksey Antropov (1716-95), on whom the traditions of the *parsuna* also had their effect. He too was active as a decorative painter, and among other work was responsible for the decoration of the Cathedral of St Andrew in Kiev during the 1750s.

At one time Antropov was principal artist to the Holy Synod, in which capacity he supervised the work of the icon-painters and did a fair amount of icon-painting himself. Inevitably this had an effect on his portraits, in which the older ideas are still strongly reflected. As an example of his work we may take his portrait of "Ataman Krasnoshchekov" (Russian Museum) *(Plate p. 257)*, which shows the rigidity of pose and concern with ornament characteristic of the *parsuna*. Krasnoshchekov's garments are adorned with a flowered brocade pattern, painted flatly with no attempt at a three-dimensional effect, and his face, with its prominent eyes and curving moustaches, is rigid and almost expressionless.

There are also some portraits by Antropov in a freer style, less subject to the influence of the *parsuna*.

Another very gifted artist of this period was Ivan Argunov (1727-1802). He was a serf of the Sheremetev family, and his career is a reminder of the difficulties and hardships besetting any serfs who showed talent in one direction or another. There were composers, actors, architects and artists of considerable quality who, as serfs, had received training at their masters' expense, but were completely without civil rights and could be sold or exchanged at their owner's whim like ordinary goods or chattels. The consequences were frequently tragic, involving the destruction of a promising talent. The history of Russian art in this period is full of cases of this kind.

Ivan Argunov suffered all the difficulties and tribulations of a serf in this situation, compelled to humour his master's every whim. Many of his portraits had to be painted from a model, for the great magnates of the day thought it beneath their dignity to sit for a portrait painted by a serf, even when he was a gifted artist. When Argunov was at the height of his powers he was transferred by the Sheremetev family from St Petersburg to Moscow to be the majordomo of their palace there, and in consequence had to devote his energies to domestic business and almost abandoned painting.

Argunov's portraits show the same transitional features as those of his contemporaries. In his early works the older conceptions of form are still prominent, but as time went on his style gained in depth and showed increased delicacy and technical skill. Thus in his portrait of Princess Lobanov-Rostovsky

the static and ornamental elements are predominant, but in the portraits of an unknown sculptor and his wife (Russian Museum) and even more strikingly in his "Peasant in Russian Costume" (Tretyakov Gallery) Argunov shows affinities with the leading artists of the second half of the century. In these works he achieves much greater freedom and independence as an artist, in his striving to reach the fullest understanding of the character of his sitters. Argunov's development is very characteristic of the period as a whole: Russian portrait painting was making steady progress towards an understanding of human psychology and was now able to convey more accurately than ever before the essence of a sitter's character and disposition.

In 18th century Russia there was one flourishing branch of art which has now fallen into decline — the art of preparing and organising festivities and celebrations of all kinds. Prodigies of skill were lavished on triumphal buildings, arches, pavilions, masquerades, and above all on fireworks. There is plentiful evidence of all this in contemporary pictures and prints, and also in the memoirs and letters of the period. The leading poets, writers and artists of the day took part in the organisation of these festivities, devoting all the resources of their imagination and taste to the creation of a splendid ceremonial occasion.

One characteristic and important genre of Russian art is represented by the popular prints known as *lubki* (in the singular *lubok*), which appeared for the first time in the second half of the 17th century and rapidly became popular with the mass of the population. These cheap prints, containing an easily intelligible text, often of a satirical character and sometimes devoted to actual events of the day, found a ready sale and penetrated into the remotest corners of the country.

The *lubki* were printed from wood blocks and then coloured. Their crudeness of style was well adapted to the tastes of their audience, and the text was frequently phrased in the language of the Russian folk tales. They were not merely a source of comfort and education for the ordinary people of Russia but were themselves works of folk art, being produced by craftsmen who belonged to the people. It was in the 18th century that they achieved their greatest flowering.

An event of great significance in the history of Russian art in the 18th century was the foundation of the Academy of Arts in St Petersburg in 1757.

The need for a professional art school had been acutely felt as early as the beginning of the 18th century. Until then there had been no centralised arrangements for the training of artists, which had been left to a variety of local groups or "teams" of artists, as they were called. At the beginning of the century there had been a school attached to the St Petersburg printing-house, and at a later stage art classes were organised by the Academy of Science; but these were merely expedients which did not meet the real need. It was essential to have a proper art school, a single establishment responsible for providing training for students in the various arts and crafts.

The Russian Academy was established in 1757 and very rapidly developed into one of the leading art schools of the world. It achieved unquestioned authority, the results of its work received general recognition, and it was no accident that some of its students who were sent to France and Italy with State bursaries were elected to honorary membership of the leading European academies of art.

The organiser of the Russian Academy was Ivan Shuvalov, an enlightened statesman and one of the most cultured men of his day, and its inspiration came from the great Russian scholar Mikhaylo Lomonosov. The 18th century was of course much concerned with education, and took a great interest in the various experiments through which it was hoped to evolve a rational and effective educational system; and Russian thinkers also were much exercised about the possibility of developing a form of teaching which should make it possible to "educate a new race of men free from the vices of contemporary society". With this in mind a training school was attached to the Academy, to which boys were admitted at the age of five or six. They remained at the school for fifteen years, following a curriculum which included education in general subjects but was principally devoted to the teaching of art.

To begin with a number of foreigners — Le Lorrain, Lagrenée, Torelli — were enlisted as teachers. Unfortunately they devoted too much time to private commissions and not enough to their teaching duties, and within two years gave up their posts, leaving nothing to show for their passage. A greater contribution was made by the French sculptor Nicolas Gillet, whose studio turned out a group of distinguished sculptors. A decisive part in the establishment of art teaching in Russia was also played by Anton Losenko, a historical painter. After the early years teaching posts at the Academy were occupied by such outstanding artists as Shubin, Martos, Gordeev, Kozlovsky, Akimov, Ugryumov, Levitsky and Kokorinov, among many others.

Throughout the 18th century the authority of the Russian Academy stood high. It maintained close connections with various foreign academies and could count among its members many European artists and writers of the highest eminence such as Boucher, Falconet and Diderot. It was not merely the leading professional school but a vital centre of artistic life, since it included within its membership almost all the Russian artists of any importance, and thus exercised a very considerable influence on the artistic life of Russia.

The Flowering of Eighteenth Century Art

The second half of the 18th century is a period of great interest in the history of Russian art, a period when many great painters, sculptors and architects were at the height of their powers, in which a whole new school of artists came to maturity.

It was also a period of important developments in both the internal and external affairs of Russia. In foreign affairs it saw the conclusion of the Seven Years' War, the partition of Poland and the recovery of Russian territory in western Belorussia, and the war with Turkey, then in an expansionist mood. The victories of Russian arms on both land and sea greatly enhanced the country's international prestige.

The internal history of Russia during this period was no less eventful. Throughout the century there were recurrent "troubles", and there was a persistent current of unrest over the evils of serfdom.

Catherine II directed all her efforts to strengthening the feudal nobility, granting them far-reaching privileges, and the serfs lost any claim to government protection. "In the eyes of the law the peasants were dead" : Radishchev's phrase was entirely apt.

The inevitable consequence of this policy was the Peasant War, the rising led by Emelyan Pugachëv. The events of the war, which shook the Empire and were followed with eager interest by the whole of Russia, represented an important stage in the struggle against the enslavement of the peasants. The more liberal elements among the nobility were powerless to make any effective contribution to the solution of the peasant problem. References to the hardships of the peasants are found in the works of many writers and poets of this period: for example, we find Mikhail Chulkov, Vladimir Lukin, Fëdor Emin and — most significantly of all — Denis Fonvizin and Nikolay Novikov attacking the arbitrary behaviour of the landowners and describing the grievous slavery to which the peasants were reduced.

There was a striking contrast between the unbridled luxury of the feudal aristocracy and the destitution of the ordinary people. Something like 800,000 serfs were distributed by Catherine to members of the nobility; and the nobles were also granted numerous privileges which ensured their loyal support for the autocratic Imperial regime.

A further scourge which afflicted the country at this period was the swarm of royal favourites. Catherine had a whole series of such favourites, who enriched themselves at the country's expense, receiving presents in the form of large estates and thousands of State-owned peasants. The Orlov brothers alone received more than 50,000 peasants from Catherine at various times.

Moreover the feudal nobility's pursuit of luxury was combined with a contempt for all things Russian, and their emulation of foreign fashions caused great harm to the development of the national culture.

The sixties and early seventies of the 18th century represented the first stage in the Russian "Enlightenment", when men like Yakov Kozelsky, Nikolay Novikov and Nikolay Kurganov were actively engaged in the movement.

In the 1770s the figurative arts took a great stride forward. New genres were established, the principles of realism triumphed in painting and sculpture, and the historical genre made important progress. The artist's concern to lay bare man's inmost nature, to comprehend his character and produce a true likeness in painting or sculpture was paralleled by the efforts being made by the thinkers of the Enlightenment to achieve recognition of the materialistic approach to knowledge and to establish a system of human values which transcended class. The association between the Enlightenment and the arts is so evident that even the gulf between literature and journalism on the one hand and painting and sculpture on the other creates no obstacle to an understanding of the essential unity of this process in the history of Russian culture.

Argunov, Rokotov, Levitsky, Shubin and Losenko — each in his own way according to the measure of his talent — penetrated into the inmost essence of human character, studied all its varied aspects, and produced portraits informed by a profound humanist understanding which achieve a powerful effect not only by their external resemblance but by their intensity of inner life. The central figure in 18th century Russian art, the embodiment of its social and aesthetic ideal, became the living, thinking human being.

Eighteenth century Russian art had close links with the art of the other peoples who formed part of the Russian Empire. The capital of the country, St Petersburg, attracted many gifted artists, who were trained in the Academy of Arts and then either returned to their home district to work or found employment in the capital. There were particularly strong and fruitful links between Russia and the Ukraine. Many Ukrainians received their professional training in Russia, and some of them subsequently made their contribution to Russian culture: we need only think, for example, of Dmitry Levitsky, Vladimir Borovikovsky and Ivan Martos. The community of interest between the various peoples was quite evident. It is important to note, however, that this was not a one-sided process in which Russian art influenced the art of the other peoples, but a constant two-way interchange. Ukrainian art, for example, had considerable influence on the art of Russia: thus the development of Russian portrait painting in the 18th century shows clear evidence of influence from the Ukrainian school of portrait painting. And this is true in varying degree of the art of the other peoples of Russia.

According to 18th century ideas the supreme artistic genre was the historical genre. The representation of the heroes of the past was accepted as the noblest task of the artist, for the exploits of these heroes overshadowed the deeds of contemporaries and were well calculated to inspire a sense of patriotism, respect for the achievements of the past, love of country, and noble and lofty sentiments. Every encouragement was therefore given to the development of historical painting and sculpture, and the work of practitioners in these genres was extravagantly praised. In comparison with this work the arts of portrait and landscape painting were regarded as being of secondary importance.

The origins of the historical genre — which at this time was widely defined to include mythological and religious as well as purely historical themes — are to be sought in the work of the Academy of Arts during the second half of the century.

The first, and the most important, figure in the field of historical painting was Anton Losenko (1737-73). Born in the Ukraine, he became a boy chorister in a court choir, and later was taken into Argunov's studio. He remained only a year in the Academy and then spent some years in France and Italy. On his return he painted two pictures − "Vladimir and Rogneda", on a theme from Russian history, and "Hector's Farewell to Andromache", on a theme from the *Iliad*. Both pictures now seem to us to contain many archaic features, but in their day they made a great impression as the first paintings in modern Russian art devoted to particular narrative themes. Losenko's works, and particularly his life studies, were admired for their perfection of technique and were frequently used as models by students in the Academy.

252

The distinctive feature of Losenko's work is his concern with Russian subject matter, and his special achievement is to have established the status of the historical genre as the highest expression of the painter's art. We have already noted his importance as a teacher; and he was also one of the most accomplished draughtsmen of his day.

The main achievements of 18th century Russian art, however, were in the field of portraiture. During this period Russian portrait painters enormously extended their technical range and their ability to reveal all the complexities of human character. Compared with the figures depicted by the historical painters, with their considerable element of abstraction and conventionality, portrait painting was an art of great vitality, pulsating with life and infinitely varied. This was the genre which surpassed all others in expressing the manifold facets of human personality. The process of establishing the value of personality in opposition to the art of the Middle Ages, which had begun in the 17th century, reached its logical culmination in the art of the portrait painters of the second half of the 18th.

Fëdor Rokotov was one of the outstanding painters of the second half of the century. Until recently his name was surrounded by an aura, if not of mystery at least of ignorance. During the 19th century he was almost forgotten. The private collections of many noble families no doubt contained paintings by this very individual artist — portraits, now dark with age, of men and women belonging to an era long past. The patina of time concealed the qualities of Rokotov's work from later generations: collectors took no interest in his paintings, and no one seems to have made any effort to discern the real gifts which they displayed.

Then all of a sudden, at the turn of the 19th and 20th centuries, Rokotov's work was rediscovered and aroused enthusiastic interest among art lovers. His pictures were displayed at exhibitions, and the public were able to appreciate their strikingly individual use of colour, their originality of manner and their technical accomplishment. In consequence they now began to be much sought after by collectors. At that time there were only three or four of his works in the Russian Museum, the remainder being in private hands.

Until quite recently nothing was known about the artist's origins, where he received his training, the dates of his birth and death, or the story of his life; but although there are still many gaps in our knowledge of Rokotov's career there is now general agreement on his stature as one of the outstanding figures of 18th century portrait painting − an artist of great originality who played an important part in the development of the genre.

Fëdor Rokotov (1735-1808) came of a serf family, and we still do not know who gave him his first training as a painter. In 1760 he was admitted to the Academy of Arts and soon became a teacher there; but even before entering the Academy he had acquired a considerable reputation and was in great demand in St Petersburg as a portrait painter. In 1765, after being granted the title of Academician, he left St Petersburg and returned to his native Moscow, where he painted most of the works to which he owes his fame.

Rokotov was a master of the "chamber portrait" – usually a head-and-shoulders representation in which the artist's attention was concentrated on the sitter's face. We also have a number of fulldress portraits by him, including a state portrait of the Empress Catherine, the first to be painted after her coronation in Moscow. But this genre did not appeal to Rokotov, and did not bring out his finest qualities. He was most at home with the chamber portrait, and it was in works of this kind that his understanding of human character and his aesthetic principles found their fullest expression.

Rokotov's portraits are of such striking individuality that they cannot be mistaken for the work of any other artist. His basic objective was to reveal the inmost personality of the sitter, and in particular his emotional mood. The figure, lit by a soft light, is almost always shown in a lively and colourful setting, and there is often a slight smile playing round the subject's mouth. The outer corners of the eyes are emphasised by delicate brushstrokes which tone down the highlights and give the sitter's glance a certain reticence and emotional force. While fully preserving the individuality of the sitter's features Rokotov is concerned to bring out his intelligence and sensibility. We can see this in his portraits of Vasily Maykov, the writer (1765, Tretyakov Gallery) *(Plate p. 247 above right)*, A. Vorontsov (1760s, Tretyakov Gallery), N. Struysky (1772, Tretyakov Gallery), Surovtsev (1780, Russian Museum) and many others.

Rokotov was particularly skilled in the painting of women. His female figures radiate a sense of virtue and purity, of dignity and humanity ; and yet behind the simplicity and naturalness of their smile there is almost always an element of mystery, a hidden significance which gives the portrait the distinctive touch we recognise as characteristic of Rokotov's work. Among the best of his female portraits are those of Mme Struysky (1772, Tretyakov Gallery), Mme Surovtsev (1780s, Russian Museum), Mme Orlov (1779, Tretyakov Gallery), Mme Santi (1785, Russian Museum) *(Plate p. 258)* and Mme Novosiltsev (1780s, Tretyakov Gallery).

Rokotov's portraits always show a very individual use of colour and rendering of material. The broadcloth and velvet of a man's waistcoat, the embroidery on his coat, the lace or gauze of his jabot, and the satin and silk of a woman's dress are painted with swift and delicate brush-strokes. In his handling of material Rokotov is not concerned to lay any particular stress on the outlines; but there is no loss of solidity, since the substance of the material is expressed by skilful use of pure painting techniques. In this respect Rokotov stands out from his contemporaries.

Rokotov thus achieved a new and important advance in the art of portrait painting, gaining an insight into the world of human personality and revealing the spiritual beauty and perfection to which it can attain.

A contemporary of Rokotov's who also gained a great reputation as a portrait painter was Dmitry Levitsky. His work is an important contribution to 18th century Russian realism and represents a considerable advance in the development of the genre. Although in the second half of the century, as in earlier years, a number of foreign portrait painters were at work in Russia — including in particular Louis Tocqué, Georg Groot, Pietro Rotari and Stefano Torelli — there were fewer of these incomers than in the first half of the century. In this period, therefore, the achievement of Russian artists takes on quite different dimensions. Their considerable technical accomplishment, their accumulated experience and their high professional standards enabled many of them to vie with the accepted foreign masters of the day. One Russian artist who not only bore comparison with foreign artists but surpassed many of them in skill was Levitsky, a magnificent draughtsman and painter who in the course of his long life painted a whole series of portraits which reflected the spirit of the age and recorded for posterity the likeness of many of his contemporaries.

Dmitry Levitsky (1735-1822) was born in the Ukraine, the son of an engraver, and received his first professional training from his father. Then in the 1750s, when the Cathedral of St Andrew in Kiev was being decorated by a group of artists under the direction of Antropov, the young Levitsky was included in the team. Subsequently he moved to St Petersburg, where he continued to be a pupil of Antropov's. He made his debut as a portrait painter at an exhibition in the Academy of Arts in 1770, when he showed a number of portraits, including one of Aleksandr Kokorinov, the architect who was also Director of the Academy *(Plate p. 247 below right)*. The professional mastery shown in this work, its fine draughtsmanship, its accuracy in reproducing the likeness of the sitter and the skill with which it gave naturalness to an official portrait were immediately recognised and acclaimed. Levitsky thereupon received official recognition, being elected an Academician and appointed professor of portrait painting. During the 1770s he reached the peak of his powers. It was at this period that he painted the small but very expressive portrait of Diderot *(Plate p. 261)*, who had come to St Petersburg on the invitation of Catherine II. Evidently Diderot himself thought highly of this picture, for he took it with him when he returned to France and it was the only portrait which he left to his sister in his will.

Levitsky is particularly known for his series of portraits of pupils at the Smolny Institute, a school for daughters of the nobility. He painted each of them in a different pose according to her particular interests: Mademoiselle Borshchov dancing, Mademoiselle Molchanov reading, Mademoiselle Alymov playing the harp. These portraits finally consolidated the artist's reputation, and henceforth he was recognised as the leading Russian portrait painter of the day.

In his portraits of members of the nobility or of friends or relatives Levitsky achieved not only an external likeness of the sitter but also an expression of his inmost being. He sought always to depict as exactly as possible the sitter's character and social position as well as his physical appearance. Thus in his portrait of the Empress's favourite, Lansky (1782, Russian Museum), Levitsky creates the image of a spoiled and empty-headed young man: behind the external magnificence depicted in this official portrait he lays bare the futility and fatuity of the sitter. But where Levitsky is dealing with a person of more substance, or one with whom he feels greater affinity, he seeks to bring out as fully as possible the warmth and humanity of the sitter. We can see this, for example, in his portraits of his daughter Agafya and his father, and in portraits of N.A. Lvov (1789, Tretyakov Gallery), N.I. Novikov (1797, Tretyakov Gallery) and M.I. Dmitriev (Tretyakov Gallery).

Levitsky's female portraits are full of charm. He painted many portraits of women, and in all of them, with his accustomed mastery, he succeeds in revealing fresh aspects of their character, new facets of their psychology. One of his most delightful works is his portrait of Mme Dyakov (1778, Tretyakov Gallery). Levitsky's acute observation of character is also seen in his portraits of Mme Naryshkin (1774, Louvre), Mme Arsentyev (1782, Louvre), Mme Bakunin (1782, Tretyakov Gallery), Mme Golitsyn (1781, Russian Museum), and many others.

The famous state portrait of Catherine II as a lawgiver, painted in the early 1780s (Tretyakov Gallery), enjoyed great popularity in its day. The majestic figure of the Empress, wearing a white satin dress, is shown against the background of a crimson canopy, standing at an altar, behind which is a marble statue representing an allegorical figure of Justice. The portrait is painted with consummate artistry, with a broad free brush, giving it a monumental unity and impressiveness appropriate to the subject. Levitsky's conception, which was enthusiastically acclaimed by contemporaries, idealised the Empress but at the same time depicted her as a representative of enlightened monarchy, the rôle in which she strove to appear in the eyes of the world.

Levitsky was one of the group of artists who in the second half of the 18th century definitively established Russian art, and portrait painting in particular, as a profoundly realistic art and set a high standard of professional competence. His work can stand beside the great masterpieces of European portrait painting: Russian portraiture, which had taken its first timid steps in the early years of the century, had now attained full maturity.

The third of the great Russian portrait painters of the second half of the century was Vladimir Borovikovsky (1757-1825). Like Levitsky, he was born in the Ukraine. In his youth he was an officer in the army, but later resigned his commission and devoted himself entirely to painting. He received his first training from his father, who was a painter, and began his career by painting icons, mural paintings in churches, and portraits. It is thought that he may have spent some time as a pupil of Levitsky's. At the end of the 1780s he arrived in St Petersburg, and the most fruitful period of his career began. His characteristic manner, the originality of his composition and his delicate sense of colour soon gained him a considerable reputation.

In the 1790s Borovikovsky created a very individual type of female portrait. The essential feature of this was the placing of the figure, usually a head-and-shoulders portrait, against a landscape background. These portraits of the 1790s, lyrical in mood and full of strong poetic feeling, are the painter's finest works.

As an example of this style we may take the portrait of Mademoiselle Lopukhin (1797, Tretyakov Gallery) *(Plate p. 262)*. The figure of the sitter, posed in front of a sunlit landscape, is full of the charm of youth and radiant with warm feeling. The slight smile playing round her lips and the demure glance suggest the tenderness and grace of her very feminine personality. In this work the artist shows great subtlety in expressing the lyrical mood of his model; and the effect is enhanced by the way in which

258

he stresses the link between the young girl and the serene sunny landscape. This was a device of which Borovikovsky was very fond and which can be seen in many of his portraits.

The use of colour in this portrait is very characteristic of Borovikovsky's style. The combination of white, blue and pink in heightened tonality is a regular feature of his work, often achieving a powerful resonance. Sometimes his use of colour is reminiscent of the ceramic-painter or the miniaturist. It can also be a very effective means of suggesting the personality of his female sitters and bringing out their lyrical mood, their femininity and their charm.

The portrait of Mademoiselle Lopukhin is one of Borovikovsky's finest works, but there are many others of similar quality. The same subtlety in the rendering of the sitter's mood is seen in his portrait of Mademoiselle Arsenyev (1790s, Russian Museum) *(Plate p. 263)*, a saucy young lady in a straw hat holding the traditional apple in her hand. There are many similar portraits, for the artist's style and composition were evidently popular with his public. Within this pattern, however, Borovikovsky nevertheless contrived to suggest the varying characters and moods of his sitters—as we can see, for example, from his portraits of Mme Skobeev, Mademoiselle Dolgoruky and a peasant girl called Khristina from the town of Torzhok.

In the 1790s Russian literature came under the influence of the sentimental school which is particularly associated with the name of Karamzin. The arts were not affected by the movement to any great extent, and few traces of its influence can be found in the work of the artists of this period. To a limited degree, however, the art of portrait painting did show some reflection of this style. The influence of the sentimental school can perhaps be traced most clearly in certain of Borovikovsky's portraits in which the elegiac and poetic mood is particularly stressed—for example in his portraits of the Gagarin sisters and the Kurakin sisters.

Borovikovsky's male portraits strike an austerer note. They are less concerned to achieve a poetic effect, they show a more positive effort to reveal the inmost character of the sitter, and they have more variety of compositional pattern. Examples are the striking portrait of the Persian Prince Murtaza-Kuli-Khan, a heavily bearded figure in Oriental costume (Russian Museum), the merciless representation of the complacent Prince A. Kurakin, the "diamond prince", and the dashing figure of General Borovsyk, painted against the background of a battle scene.

In addition to his portraits Borovikovsky also did much religious painting. In particular he took part in the decoration of the Cathedral of Our Lady of Kazan in St Petersburg. This work did not, however, compare in importance with his portrait painting. He was one of the three great artists of the second half of the 18th century who enhanced the significance of the realistic portrait, emancipated it from the archaic features inherited from the past, and established the importance of the genre. During the 18th century Russian portrait painting had come a long way: starting from the rigid conventions of the *parsuna*, it had progressed towards a profound understanding of human nature and had shown itself able to depict all the complexities of human personality—the most difficult task with which an artist can be faced.

Rokotov, Levitsky and Borovikovsky were by no means the only painters of quality in the second half of the 18th century, but their great gifts and their technical virtuosity made them outstanding among their contemporaries. Their work had a great influence on the subsequent development of portrait painting in the 19th century.

Another genre which developed in the second half of the century was the art of landscape painting. This genre had indeed existed at an earlier stage in the development of Russian art — in the decorative painting and engraving of the first half of the century, for example — but in this earlier period it had been of secondary importance, sometimes no more than a form of applied art. Now, however, a group of landscape artists trained in the Academy of Arts raised the status of the genre to new heights. This development of landscape painting was connected with the new romantic attitude to nature which was characteristic of the period. At first, it is true, the genre was marked by a certain artificiality; but in the work of its leading practitioners it attained a high degree of expressiveness and truth to nature.

The founder of the new genre was Semën Shchedrin (1745-1804), who had received his training in the Academy. In his pictures he depicted the parks and palaces of Pavlovsk, Gatchina, Peterhof and St Petersburg itself. His landscapes were usually built up on the basis of linear perspective, with the view framed between lateral features in the foreground. The use of colour was fairly conventional, with warm tones of brown predominating in the foreground, different shades of green in the middle distance, and cold blue tones in the background. This conventionality of colouring is found in most of the painters of the period, though there are certain exceptions to the rule. One of these who must be referred to is Fëdor Alekseev (1753-1824), a highly gifted artist who produced some fine views of St Petersburg. His pictures show a livelier use of colour, and his landscapes are inhabited by real people, the ordinary citizens of the town going about their everyday business, which gives his paintings a great feeling of naturalness. Moreover, like other landscapists, he had a good eye for the shapes of buildings and for architectural detail, and faithfully recorded the new construction then taking place in St Petersburg.

But the new landscape painters did more than produce accurate pictures of many attractive corners of the Russian countryside: they also demonstrated the vitality and significance of the art of landscape painting, established its status as an independent genre, and prepared the way for its further development in the 19th century.

Even in the art of mediaeval Russia we find some elements of genre painting in icons and mural paintings. In depicting scenes from ordinary life these earlier artists showed their interest in reflecting everyday reality and their dissatisfaction with an exclusively religious subject matter, seeking to give life to the imaginary events they depicted by showing the characters of the scriptural stories in real surroundings which would be familiar and comprehensible to the spectator.

The 18th century saw the emergence of genre painting as it is generally understood. In the middle of the century Ivan Firsov painted his picture of "The Young Painter", showing a young artist at his easel painting the portrait of a girl, perhaps his sister. The representation of the figures and the accurate rendering of the room and the still life on the table suggest that the picture was painted from life, and show an acute sense of observation. "The Young Painter" is a genre picture in the full meaning of the term.

Artists now began to show a lively interest in peasant life and manners. Foreign artists had long been aware of the rich store of subject matter to be found in Russia — the idiosyncrasies of Russian character, the manners and customs of the people, the landscape. This is exemplified by the work of the French painter Jean Le Prince, who spent some years in Russia and painted a series of pictures of peasant life. Le Prince's work, however, was exceedingly remote from reality. What interested him was the exotic aspect of Russian life and manners, and in consequence his work lost all naturalness and truth to life. The peasant costumes became merely stage properties, the peasants themselves were mere lay figures, and scenes of everyday life were transformed into rather stilted pastorals. The result was quite without artistic value, as contemporaries noted: "The whole thing is cold, colourless, without expression," Diderot wrote about Le Prince's work.

Russian artists were, of course, better acquainted with the circumstances of peasant life under serfdom. A complete absence of civil rights, destitution, absolute dependence on the landowners — these were the realities of peasant life. To give artistic expression to these things was beyond the powers of the newly-fledged Russian realist school: this was a task reserved for the 19th century. But in the first half of the 18th century many painters took their subject matter from peasant life. One painter who dealt directly with this theme was Mikhail Shibanov, himself a serf belonging to the statesman G. A. Potëmkin. In one of his paintings, "The Peasants' Dinner", he showed a peasant family gathered round a table at their meagre meal. In this work, it is true, there is still no profound revelation of character; but at least the attempt had been made.

In another picture, "The Betrothal", Shibanov shows a party of peasants engaged in celebrating this traditional ceremony, a variegated group drawn together by the solemnity of the occasion and by the bond of tradition. The scene is depicted without embellishment; and we know from an inscription by the painter on the picture that it was painted from life.

The theme of peasant life was handled in an individual way by one of the most original and gifted artists of the 18th century, Ivan Ermenëv (1746 to after 1792). He had an unusual career, which is known to us only in the broadest outline. The son of a stableman who became a student at the Academy of Arts and was sent to Paris with a bursary from the Academy, Ermenëv was a witness of the French Revolution and recorded the fall of the Bastille in one of a series of drawings which were later engraved. Some of his allegorical pictures acquired a certain reputation, but it is not these that make him an important figure in the history of Russian art.

Returning to Russia, Ermenëv painted a series of water colours of peasant types. In these works there is no trace of the pastoral manner: they show the poor destitute wretches who were commonly to be met with on the roads of Russia in those days. One picture depicts a peasant dinner, and is in complete contrast to Shibanov's work. It shows the bare and comfortless log walls of a peasant *izba* and a crudely made table with a peasant family sitting silently round it eating hungrily out of a single dish, an expression of infinite weariness and foreboding on their faces. Another picture shows a group of blind beggars singing in a market-place -- sitting in a circle dolefully intoning a melancholy song in the hope of attracting alms.

In a similar style are a series of drawings showing beggars and blind men travelling the roads with their knapsacks. These usually show one or two figures clad in filthy rags and tatters and carrying staffs in their hands, sometimes under the conduct of a leader, or single figures tramping from village to village in search of charity. They are depicted against a low horizon, which gives the figures increased significance and brings out more forcibly the tragedy of their situation.

All these pictures share the same artistic intention, and Ermenëv clearly demonstrates his sympathy with these outcasts in the hardships they have to endure. The drawings were done in the 1770s, at a time when many who had taken part in Pugachëv's unsuccessful peasant rising were still roaming aimlessly about the countryside. Not all of the drawings were finished, but all of them are clearly and carefully drawn — and all of them are a cry from the artist's heart.

We know little of Ermenëv's later career, but it seems to have ended tragically. After a further stay in France he returned to Russia, and appears to have died destitute and forgotten.

Russian genre painting was thus a creation of the 18th century. Slowly at first, but steadily, artists developed an interest in the life of ordinary people, and their work increased in quality and profundity. They thus prepared the way for the important development of genre painting in the early 19th century in the work of Aleksey Venetsianov and his school.

The second half of the 18th century also saw the formation of the Russian classical school. In the circumstances of Russian life it was natural that men should feel an urgent desire to set up a lofty ideal, a standard of perfection which was free from the sordidness of ordinary life and recalled the virtues of the great men of antiquity. The task of art was now to provide an education in citizenship and to promote patriotism, a sense of moral and public duty, and other civic virtues. The quest for perfect artistic models which should achieve these objectives led quite naturally to a remote period of antiquity, and to an art centred on the ideal of the free and harmoniously developed human being.

The classical style achieved its fullest expression in France, where its birth can be dated to the end of the 1760s and the early 1770s. During these years the last surviving remnants of the Rococo, the *rocaille* style, came under heavy attack, and the principles of the new school were established.

To the 18th century classicists ancient Greece and Rome were no mere fabulous world, and classicism itself was by no means an attempt to seek refuge in antiquity from the perplexing problems of contemporary life. Antiquity was thought of as an entirely concrete historical reality. No one doubted that the heroes of the Greeks and Romans had actually existed; no one questioned the existence of the free society in which they had lived and which had nurtured their heroic virtues. The remote past was seen as a fortunate period in human history, but a very real period which had been reflected in an out-pouring of perfect works of art. The world of the Bible was full of abstraction and unreality, but the world of antiquity was a real period in human history which had a meaning for the men of the modern world.

The culmination of the classical school in France was reached in the work of Louis David, with its profound social implications. His "Oath of the Horatii", "Death of Marat" and other remarkable works give expression to the progressive philosophy which was at the basis of the classical style.

Classicism developed in Russia at almost the same time as in France. In spite of the artificiality of dividing the history of art into periods, and the perennial controversies to which any attempt to do so gives rise, the origins of this style in Russia can reasonably be dated to the end of the sixties and the early seventies of the 18th century. The change can be clearly detected in architecture, sculpture and painting, in works by Vallin de la Mothe, Kokorinov, Gordeev, Losenko, Martos and Kozlovsky, among others, which show that the characteristics of the new school had not only attained a certain stability but had been welded into a recognisable unity of style.

Classicism in Russia was a style of great vigour and creative force which made a deep and lasting impression on Russian art. In the second half of the 18th century its influence was felt in every branch of art. Painting and sculpture, architecture and applied art, engraving and drawing — each of these genres, in varying degree, was caught up in the trend, and few indeed were the artists of the period who escaped the influence of the new style.

Russian classicism, however, was not in any sense a borrowing from the West. It was no mere import from Paris or Rome, brought back by travellers as the *dernier cri* of foreign fashion. It emerged in Russia as a necessary stage in the development of the national culture, as a logical consequence of the lofty objectives towards which progressive social and aesthetic thought in Russia was directed.

The influence of classicism was particularly marked in architecture, which succeeded in embodying the traditions inherited from antiquity in a characteristically national style of building. The process of development of the new style can be seen most clearly, therefore, in the field of architecture, where classicism launched a vigorous offensive against the Baroque, and the new principles rapidly found expression in the buildings of what is known as the "transitional period".

The days of remote antiquity were conceived as a time of freedom and independence for man, a time in which he was able to achieve the harmonious development of his personality and was free from the shackles of oppression. The real situation of the various social groups in the ancient world — the slavery, the predatory wars — was totally ignored. Russian artists were well acquainted with the history of ancient Rome and Greece: they had been familiar with it since their childhood, and they knew all about the heroes of antiquity and their exploits. Their vision of ancient history, however, took account only of its most striking aspects, seeing it as a period which attained a supreme development of human personality, which created magnificent works of architecture and plastic art, which set a standard of high artistic achievement.

Russian classicism gave expression to the quest for social harmony, the lack of which was so clearly evident in Russia. The heroes of antiquity, those dwellers in a remote golden age, were seen as the antithesis to the bitter injustices and hardships of contemporary Russia. Just as in revolutionary France the classical style was adopted by the opponents of absolutism, providing them with the heroic attitudes and slogans in which they expressed their revolutionary fervour, so in 18th century Russia it became the vehicle for the lofty ideal which the progressive elements in Russian society were striving to realise.

The principal theme of Russian classicism was man, in whom the 18th century had boundless confidence. This belief in human destiny was indeed the supreme achievement of the century.

Winckelmann's definition of the qualities of classical art, "noble simplicity and tranquil grandeur", was not unquestioningly accepted by Russian artists. The vitalising link of art with everyday reality and the material world fostered the strain of realism which permeated Russian classicism and created its special national individuality. Losenko's "Hector", Gordeev's "Prometheus", Shchedrin's "Endymion", Ugryumov's "Yan Usmar", Kozlovsky's "Yakov Dolgoruky" and "Mounted Hercules" and many other works of the second half of the 18th century had a direct relevance to life, in both ideological content and artistic form. The distinctive feature of Russian classicism was that its practitioners were concerned not only with antiquity but with the history of their native land; and it was this that gave the works of the classical school their particular strength.

It must be remembered that in the second half of the 18th century classicism was by no means the only trend in Russian art. This was also the period of Shubin, Rokotov and Levitsky, whose work shows hardly a trace of classical influences and who nevertheless were among the leading artists of the day. The art of this period accommodated both a thoroughgoing realist like Shubin and a classicist like Kozlovsky; both of these artists gave full and personal expression to the aesthetic principles of the period, and both of them — notwithstanding their differences in artistic approach and in style — were profoundly involved in the life of that period.

An important part in the development of Russian sculpture was played by the Academy of Arts, which within ten years of its establishment had produced artists of the calibre of Fedot Shubin, Fëdor Gordeev, Mikhail Kozlovsky, Ivan Martos and Feodosy Shchedrin, among many others. The Academy actively promoted the development of the different sculptural genres, giving particular attention to carving in relief, which became very popular in the 18th century.

The outstanding achievement of Russian plastic art in the second half of the century lay in the field of portrait sculpture. The enhanced status which Rokotov, Levitsky and Borovikovsky had given the painted portrait was matched by a corresponding development of the sculptured portrait. It is significant that the portrait sculpture of this period was barely touched by the influence of classicism.

270

The development of the portrait remained firmly within the traditions of realism; and however fervently an artist believed in the principles of classicism, immediately he turned to portraiture and was faced with the problem of representing the personality of a living human being in all its complexity he inevitably adopted a realistic approach.

Almost all the leading Russian sculptors of the period — Gordeev, Kozlovsky, Prokofyev, Martos and Shchedrin — were active in the field of portraiture, understood the specific requirements of the genre, and produced works of first-rate importance. The greatest contribution to the art of portrait sculpture, however, was made by Fedot Shubin (1740-1805), one of the outstanding figures in the history of Russian art.

Like Lomonosov, Shubin came from the White Sea area, and while still a boy became passionately interested in the art of carving, which was highly developed in this northern part of Russia; and after receiving his training at the Academy of Arts he retained a close link with folk art. An acute understanding of character, a remarkable psychological insight, an approach which varied according to the requirements of the particular portrait, and consummate technical skill: these are the qualities we find in Shubin's portraits. According to the aesthetic principles of the day the portrait was a genre of secondary importance; and it was Shubin, more than any of his contemporaries, who set the highest professional standards for this genre and established its aesthetic significance.

In his portrait sculpture Shubin shows a profound knowledge of life and of human character; he displays great variety and delicacy of perception, and can on occasion be quite merciless in his revelation of character. A striking example of his mature style is his portrait of Prince A. Golitsyn (1775, Tretyakov Gallery), a complex and fully rounded representation of a typical 18th century Russian magnate. Although compelled by circumstances to devote his talent to producing portraits of the feudal nobility, Shubin invariably achieves an acute and accurate insight into the character of his sitters and faithfully renders their personality and their inmost nature. This can be seen, for example, in such works as his portraits of members of the Orlov family, P. Sheremetev, G. Potëmkin, A. Bezborodko and E. Chulkov. Many of his portraits are imbued with a surprising warmth of feeling and a profound respect for his model — as, for example, in his portrait of Lomonosov (1790s, Academy of Science, Moscow) *(Plate p. 260)*, with whom he had much in common both in his career and in his attitude to life.

Shubin was one of those artists whose skill shows no sign of decline with advancing age, and only a year or two before his death he painted his famous portrait of Paul I (1801, Russian Museum), a masterpiece of Russian portrait sculpture.

Shubin's portraits reflect all the variety of Russian character in his period, covering a wide range of age, temperament, experience and social position. He was a shrewd observer with a profound understanding of human nature; and his clear-sighted artistic vision enabled him to penetrate into the inmost recesses of a man's character, laying bare the essence of his being, concealed though it might sometimes be by outward appearances.

Shubin's work occupies a prominent place in any account of 18th century Russian art because his profound psychological insight enabled him to give expression to the aesthetic ideals which were central to the art of the period. In this respect Shubin's portraits are comparable with the best work of Rokotov, Levitsky and Borovikovsky.

One of the major events in the history of Russian sculpture was the erection of Etienne Maurice Falconet's famous statue of Peter the Great, representing him in the character of a great statesman and lawgiver; and the story of its creation is significant and instructive.

Throughout the 18th century the figure of Peter the Great had attracted the interest of many artists and his image had been reproduced in numerous portraits, busts, mosaics and engravings. It had also inspired two pieces of monumental sculpture. The first of these, by Carlo Rastrelli, has already been referred to. In the 1760s it appeared rather old-fashioned: the massive figure of the Tsar in his pompous attire was reminiscent of a Roman emperor, and this severe and majestic presence was quite out of line with the contemporary assessment of Peter's character and his contribution to the development of Russia. Peter was now recognised as a great statesman and lawgiver who had transformed the whole life of Russia; and this was how the public wanted to see their hero represented. Accordingly, on the recommendation of Diderot, a new statue was commissioned from Etienne Maurice Falconet (1716-91), an accomplished sculptor though admittedly with no experience of monumental sculpture, being known chiefly for his decorative sculpture, a statue of "Milon of Croton", and his designs for the Sèvres Manufactory. In spite of this limited experience, however, Diderot was able to perceive Falconet's undeveloped creative possibilities, his high professional gifts and his acute intelligence.

Falconet had made a profound study of the Petrine period. It happened that Voltaire, the "uncrowned king of Europe", had just published his *History of Russia in the Reign of Peter the Great*, which glorified Peter as a wise statesman, the "giant of the North". This was the first serious study of Peter published in a foreign country, a work based on authentic documents and free from the anecdotes and inventions which were so commonly found in books about Peter. Falconet knew Voltaire's work and undoubtedly learned a great deal from it. In addition, as he himself tells us, the ideas of the Russian "Enlightenment" played a great part in developing his conception of Peter. In expressing this conception in his statue he strove for the utmost simplicity and economy. "I am producing a statue of this hero," he wrote to Diderot, "representing him neither as a great commander nor as a conqueror — though of course he was both of these. Much more sublime is the character of the creator, the lawgiver, the benefactor of his country; and this is the character in which he must be represented."

This was the beginning of years of unremitting effort. Falconet produced a number of variations on the theme; a huge granite boulder weighing 100,000 poods was found, with considerable trouble, to serve as a pedestal; and unusual difficulties had to be overcome in the casting of the statue. Throughout the whole course of the work, indeed, innumerable difficulties were encountered; and although Falconet the artist was able to surmount them, Falconet the man, for all his resolution and directness of character, was powerless against the envy of his rivals and the hostility of courtiers. He was assisted in his work by Russian artists and bronze-founders and enjoyed the affection and respect of his fellow craftsmen, with whom he discussed every detail of the work as it progressed. Altogether the production of the statue took more than twelve years; but when the ceremonial inauguration took place in 1782 Falconet was not present, having already returned to France.

This statue of Peter the Great — the "Bronze Horseman", as it has been called since Pushkin wrote his famous poem with this title — became the emblem of St Petersburg *(Plate p. 264 right)*. The horse rearing up on its hind legs and the commanding figure of the Emperor were seen as a symbol of the new Russia, expressed with masterly skill in a composition of striking originality.

The effect of the statue is finely conveyed in Pushkin's lines :

Darkly it looms in terrifying power :
What force of mind that brow conveys !
What mighty strength lies there concealed !
And in that horse what fire !
Whither away, thou haughty steed ?
Where shall these proud hooves bear thee now ?
And thou, lord over destiny,
Didst thou not, with iron rein,
Pull Russia, rearing high,
Back from the brink of the abyss ?

The statue conveys a powerful sense of dynamism, expressed in its soaring urgency of line and its unity of creative impulse. The horseman and the rock on which he stands are combined into a single significant whole; the bond between the statue and the pedestal here achieves a classical harmony. The simplicity and economy of the composition are matched by the simplicity and significance of the detail. The commanding gesture of Peter's right arm, full of powerful kinetic force, conveys all the nervous energy of the man. The whole conception of the statue is informed by the progressive ideology. of the Enlightenment, presenting the monarch as a wise statesman, the "first citizen" of his kingdom, the guardian of legality and the educator of his people.

Falconet had no followers in Russia; but his immortal work provided an inspiring example of supreme craftsmanship which could not but be of benefit to the rising generation of Russian artists.

The Russian sculptors of the classical school produced works of great expressive power and high artistic quality. The leading representatives of this school were Fëdor Gordeev, Ivan Prokofyev, Ivan Martos, Feodosy Shchedrin and Mikhail Kozlovsky. Some of their sculpture still shows signs of baroque influence, but in their best works they express the aesthetic ideals of classicism.

The senior member of the group was Fëdor Gordeev (1745-1810), who was known for his "Prometheus" and a number of funerary monuments. He also produced a series of copies of works of ancient sculpture in which the originals were treated with considerable freedom.

Martos's funerary monuments, Shchedrin's "Venus" and "Diana", and a number of works by Prokofyev are instinct with the spirit of classicism, reflecting a varied and significant subject matter and expressing the ideology of humanism and the artists' striving to achieve supreme plastic perfection.

The leading sculptor of the closing years of the century was Mikhail Kozlovsky (1753-1802). An artist of great creative vigour and consummate professional skill, he produced a number of works which are entitled to a prominent place in the history of Russian sculpture. Perhaps more than any other sculptor of the period he gave expression to the ideals of patriotism and the aspirations of his contemporaries. His "Mounted Hercules", "Yakov Dolgoruky", "Alexander the Great's Vigil" and other works show the powerful significance which Russian sculpture could now achieve.

Two works of outstanding importance produced by Kozlovsky shortly before his death are the statue of "Samson" in the famous Great Cascade at Peterhof and the monument to General Suvorov in Leningrad.

By the beginning of the 19th century the buildings, parks and fountains at Peterhof which had been created by Russian artists and craftsmen of the previous century had fallen into a state of neglect and dilapidation and were in need of restoration. The old lead statues which lined the cascades had also suffered from the effects of time and were on the point of complete collapse. It was decided, therefore, to replace all the statues which were beyond repair. This reconstruction of the cascade and the replacement of the old statues by new ones was an event of great importance in the history of Russian sculpture, and all the leading sculptors of the day, including Martos, Shubin, Shchedrin, Kozlovsky and Prokofyev, were enlisted in the task.

The operation was an extensive one, covering not only the casting of new statues from the old moulds but also the production of a number of new figures which transformed the whole decorative pattern of Peterhof. Prokofyev's "Perseus", "Sirens", "River Neva", and "River Volkhov", Shubin's "Pandora" and Martos's "Actaeon" enhanced the magnificence of the total effect, and the centrepiece of the whole design was provided by Kozlovsky's splendid statue of "Samson".

The figure of Samson is vibrant with inner force and commanding strength. The complex structure of this muscular body expresses infinite self-confidence, the resolution of the warrior and the triumph of the victor. His contest with the lion is interpreted by Kozlovsky in the spirit of the legendary hand-to-hand struggles which were a favourite theme of the old Russian epic tales; and this link with the traditional folk hero is reinforced by the fact that Samson is represented with the features of an ordinary Russian man of the people. Standing on an artificial rock in the centre of a basin, surrounded by the spray of the fountain, the bronze figure of Samson acquires added decorative and expressive force.

The culmination of Kozlovsky's achievement as a monumental sculptor is his statue of the great Russian commander General Suvorov. Suvorov is represented in the pose of a real folk hero, holding his sword and shield, a figure of impetuous energy. The statue shows Kozlovsky's art at the stage of full maturity and at the peak of its artistic attainment. One of the most popular works of Russian monumental art, it demonstrates the high standard of accomplishment reached by Russian sculpture and represents in effect the final culmination of the process of development which it had passed through in the course of the previous century.

The 1760s and 1770s saw considerable changes in Russian architecture. The earlier concentration on palace building was no longer in accordance with the needs of the time. The towns were continuing to increase in size, and industry and trade were developing; and this made it necessary for architecture to turn in new directions. Public buildings, industrial installations and the problems of urban layout now received particular attention, and the building of splendid and pretentious palaces was no longer the architect's principal function. The development of architecture was increasingly influenced by the ideas of the Enlightenment and by the growing social and national awareness of Russian society. The quest for a new architectural ideal led in the direction of classicism and of the forms inherited from antiquity, with its rationalism and its austere and majestic ideal of beauty.

Although the building of palaces and churches still continued, the main emphasis now shifted to urban development. A special commission was established to prepare plans for the development of the towns of Russia. The older parts of the towns were rebuilt and new quarters constructed; streets were straightened; the old fortifications were demolished; and a network of new main streets and squares was laid out. This happened not only in St Petersburg and Moscow but in many provincial towns. In this period, too, a new type of mansion − a large establishment standing in its own park − came into favour among the wealthy. The layout of the parks also changed, the old regular plan being replaced by the landscaped "English park". Formal geometric patterns gave place to the natural beauty of the countryside − even though this too might be created by the genius of the landscape gardener.

Architectural form now became increasingly dominated by the classical order, which gradually superseded the decorative features of the baroque style — though at first these continued in use.

One of the outstanding figures of these early days of classicism was the gifted architect Aleksandr Kokorinov (1726-72), who received his training in Ukhtomsky's school in Moscow and later moved to St Petersburg, where he established a thriving architectural practice. Kokorinov's finest building was the Academy of Arts, of which he was Director and the principal moving spirit during its early years. Lying on the banks of the Neva, it is notable for the originality of its internal layout, a clear-cut plan in which a large circular courtyard is enclosed within a rectangle. The main reception rooms lie along the principal front facing on to the Neva, with the studios and classrooms in the central part of the building. Kokorinov successfully solved the many problems of design arising from the use of the building for teaching — the studios, the classrooms, the exhibition halls, and so on. The serene rhythm of the façades expresses the internal structure; and the small projecting pavilions, decorated with columns, emphasise the severity of the main structure and create an impression of classical magnificence.

Another leading architect of this period was Vallin de la Mothe (1729-1800), who was invited to come to St Petersburg to teach in the Academy of Arts. He also had a part in designing the exterior of the Academy, but his talent came to full expression in the "Little Hermitage" which, in spite of its severity of line, achieved complete harmony with Rastrelli's adjoining Winter Palace. Another important building for which he was responsible was "New Holland", originally designed as a timber warehouse but never completed. The gateway, a masterpiece of disciplined form, still survives to demonstrate the architect's mastery of his craft and the characteristic features of the new style.

Also active in this period was Yury Velten (1730-1801), a prolific architect who designed many fine buildings. He was for many years credited with the planning of the famous Neva embankments, with their remarkable beauty of design and magnificence of scale; but the most recent research has shown that there is no basis for attributing this work to him. Nor is he any longer regarded as the designer of the famous grille round the Summer Garden in St Petersburg. He was responsible for the execution of these works in his capacity as chief architect of the "Building Department" which carried out all building operations in the capital. The real designer of the embankments and the grille has not yet been definitely established.

Much of the palace building carried out during these years was the work of Antonio Rinaldi (c. 1710-1794), an Italian architect who found a second home in Russia. Rinaldi's major achievement was the Chinese Palace at Oranienbaum (now Lomonosov), with lavish carved and painted decoration reminiscent of mid 18th century architecture. A much plainer building by the same architect is the Marble Palace in St Petersburg, a majestic structure faced with coloured marble and decorated with Corinthian pilasters. Certain decorative elements in this building still retain traces of the *rocaille* style of the late Rococo ; but these are restrained and unobtrusive and are subordinated to the severe lines of the overall design. The interior of the Marble Palace is also decorated with marble carving by some of the leading Russian sculptors of the day, including Shubin and Kozlovsky. The characteristic feature of Rinaldi's buildings, including his Gatchina Palace, is his concentration on decoration and ornament : to him the problems involved in the general conception and design of a building were of secondary importance.

The work of the architects we have been considering thus shows all the evidence of belonging to a period of transition when a new type of Russian architecture was in process of development. The buildings they erected became an integral part of the architectural pattern of St Petersburg, Moscow and other cities, not only giving the period a distinctive style of its own but also preparing the way for the achievements of the leading architects of the following period — Bazhenov, Kazakov and Starov. In the work of these architects Russian classicism found its fullest expression, and the buildings they designed represent the culminating point of Russian architecture in the second half of the 18th century.

The most gifted of the three was Vasily Bazhenov (1737-99), an architect of outstanding talent and great professional accomplishment. He occupies a special place in the history of Russian architecture as a man of wide culture, an apostle of the philosophy of the Enlightenment, a scholar and theoretical writer, and a great teacher. After receiving his early training in Ukhtomsky's school in Moscow he soon found his way to St Petersburg and completed his professional education in the newly established

Academy of Arts. Two years later he was sent to France and Italy, where he made a thorough study of classical architecture. The work he did during his stay in these countries revealed his considerable talent, and he was elected to membership of a number of European academies.

Returning to St Petersburg in 1765, he was appointed an Academician and prepared a design for a new Arsenal. He then went back to Moscow, and a new period of creative activity began. The most important work he produced during this period was a design for a palace in the Kremlin (1767-73). This was a grandiose plan for the erection of a great palace complex on the Kremlin hill, incorporating all the existing buildings into a pattern which included a number of open squares and grand colonnades. Bazhenov's design replaced the seclusion and privacy of the mid 18th century palaces by the new conception of a complex of buildings open to the public view. Much use was made of the Ionic order on the exterior of the palace, producing an effect of sober magnificence and monumentality. Bazhenov produced a superb model of his projected palace, which gives us some idea of the magnificence of his conception. The model is of particular value because the building was never in fact built: there was a ceremonial laying of the foundation stone, but the structure never progressed beyond this. Nevertheless Bazhenov's design had great influence on his contemporaries and made a major contribution towards establishing the principles of classicism in Russian architecture.

The principles of planning exemplified in this project represented an important and influential contribution to architectural design. Bazhenov showed equal originality in his design for a palace at Tsaritsyno on the outskirts of Moscow, in which, basing himself on the older traditions of Russian architecture, he planned a whole series of buildings to be sited in a park — an Imperial residence in the country consisting of two main ranges of buildings, together with various pavilions and summer-houses, domestic offices, a theatre and other associated buildings. The whole design is notable for its quiet elegance, the organic link between the architecture and the surrounding countryside, and the lavish decoration. Although the Empress Catherine wanted the palace to be in the Moorish Gothic style, Bazhenov followed the established traditions of Russian architecture, and it is this that gives his design its distinctive character.

The unfortunate architect, however, was dogged by misfortune. Catherine, suspecting him of a connection with the freemasons, declared the style of the building to be too sombre for her taste, had it razed to the ground, and commissioned Kazakov to design a new palace. Nevertheless the study of Bazhenov's original designs — which fortunately have been preserved — and of the other buildings in the complex still enable us to appreciate the great merits of his work.

One of Bazhenov's finest buildings was the Pashkov Palace in Moscow (1786), now the Lenin Library. The plan of the building followed the typical layout of a noble establishment, with the mansion on top of the hill and the garden on the lower slopes, surrounded by a grille. The principal reception rooms were in the main block, with living quarters in pavilions round the outside. The general composition is extremely effective: standing in a commanding position on its hill, the building looks impressive from every direction. The principles of layout are entirely traditional, recalling the technique of the older Russian architects with their unerring instinct for the siting of architectural masses in the landscape. The Pashkov Palace was one of Bazhenov's finest achievements and a magnificent addition to the townscape of Moscow.

One of the last of Bazhenov's major works was the Michael Castle (Engineers' Castle) in St Petersburg, built for Paul I. This is in the form of a closed square with an internal courtyard, and the main decorative features are on the principal façade, to which a high plinth, a portico, twin columns and sculptured decoration give a particularly imposing effect. Bazhenov died before the building was finished, and the work was completed by the Italian architect Vincenzo Brenna. Brenna departed from Bazhenov's original plan and overloaded the building with decoration, but the general character of the design was preserved. In 1800 Rastrelli's equestrian statue of Peter the Great, made half a century earlier, was erected in the square in front of the castle, where it harmonised perfectly with the façade and greatly enhanced the effect of the building.

Bazhenov was an architect of authentic greatness, whose significance extends far beyond the bounds of his century. In his layouts and designs he not only contributed to the development of the classical style and gave it distinctively Russian characteristics, but anticipated many of the ideas which were to play a central part in the architecture of later generations.

Matvey Kazakov (1738-1812) was the second of the three great architects of this period. He too received his professional training in Ukhtomsky's studio in Moscow, and then practised as an architect in Tver. His architectural education was completed by Bazhenov, whom he assisted in the designing of the Kremlin palace. Kazakov's first important work was the Petrovsky Palace (begun 1775). The design of this building — the line of the façades and the general layout — was influenced by the traditions of Russian architecture, and also betrayed the influence of Bazhenov.

In the 1770s Kazakov built the so-called "Government Offices" in the Kremlin (now occupied by the Supreme Soviet). This was planned in the form of a triangle, one side of which faced on to Red Square, enclosing a grand courtyard; but it was also an entirely new type of administrative building, planned with great economy and functional efficiency.

Kazakov's originality and professional competence were also demonstrated by his design for Moscow University, built between 1786 and 1793. In style this building was much more restrained, and it showed a great advance in the use of the order. At the end of the 1790s Kazakov built the Golitsyn Hospital in Moscow — a large complex of buildings consisting of a central block flanked by wings containing the wards. The severe Doric porticoes and the central dome are very characteristic of his style.

The third great architect of the period was Ivan Starov (1774-1808), who was also trained in the Academy of Arts. His work covered a very wide range — palaces, public and administrative buildings, churches — and he was also much concerned with urban layout. The most important of his earlier works was the Cathedral of the Trinity in the Alexander Nevsky Monastery in St Petersburg. A three-aisled basilica in plan, the Cathedral has a severe Doric hexastyle portico and is crowned by a dome and two bell-towers. Even this early work showed Starov's remarkable gifts and in particular his understanding of the classical order.

In his later years Starov was responsible for a palace at Pella, a mansion on the estate of Sivoritsa (both on the outskirts of Leningrad), and other buildings; but his outstanding achievement was the Tauride Palace in St Petersburg (1783-89) *(Plate p. 264 middle left)*, built for Prince G. Potëmkin. In this building he adopts a severely classical style, incorporating the Doric order, observing strict restraint in the design of the main structure, and emphasising the flatness of the walls. The central block extends back from the façade, with the lateral wings enclosing a grand courtyard which is cut off from the street by a grille. The interior of the palace, the internal colonnades and the sculptured decoration are of superlative effect.

Bazhenov, Kazakov and Starov thus made a considerable mark on their period, producing buildings which not only demonstrated their own professional mastery but also made an outstanding contribution to Russian architecture and to the successful establishment of the principles of classicism.

These three architects did not, however, stand alone. Many others, both Russian and foreign, were active in this period, all making their contribution to the development of Russian architecture. Among them was Nikolay Lvov.

Nikolay Lvov (1751-1803), a man of wide culture — a poet, composer and scholar as well as a very gifted architect — is principally known as the designer of the Post Office in St Petersburg. The clearly articulated design of the basement storey, the severe pilasters on the first floor and the functional planning of the building demonstrate the architect's technical mastery and his remarkable sense of style. It was to buildings such as this that St Petersburg owed its severely classical lines and its unique beauty. Lvov is also known as the designer of the Neva Gate in the Fortress of SS. Peter and Paul, a work of classical restraint which harmonises perfectly with the plainness of the walls. Lvov's activities were not, however, confined to St Petersburg: among the many buildings outside the capital for which he was responsible the most important is the cathedral in Torzhok, a large building in the classical style with five domes.

The Italian architect Giacomo Quarenghi (1744-1817) was another foreigner who found a second home in Russia, coming to St Petersburg in 1779 and remaining there until his death. He was well versed in the traditions of Russian architecture, which had a great influence on his work and played a part in the design of many buildings which gave clear expression to the principles of Russian classicism.

One of Quarenghi's early works was the Academy of Science in St Petersburg, situated on the banks of the Neva (1787). The pillared portico, the clearly defined granite basement storey and the staircase leading to the main entrance underline the restrained simplicity of the design of the façade.

From the beginning Quarenghi's work shows a striving towards sobriety of form and the most effective use of the order. During the 1780s he also built the Hermitage Theatre, fitting it so skilfully into the architectural ensemble on the Neva embankment that in spite of the difference in style it combined with the Winter Palace to form a unified whole. Here again Quarenghi emphasises the separateness of the basement storey, linking the two upper stories with a Corinthian colonnade.

All Quarenghi's work shows the same delicacy of proportion in the details — the doors and windows, the cornices, and so on. One of his most important buildings is the Assignation Bank in Sadovy Street, a complex and skilfully designed structure consisting of a central block linked by an open colonnade to a long semicircular gallery. In the central block the Corinthian order is used.

Quarenghi's mastery was also displayed in the English Palace at Peterhof and the Aleksandrovsky Palace at Pushkin. Unfortunately the English Palace was destroyed by German forces during the second world war, but the Aleksandrovsky Palace is still one of the attractions of the town of Pushkin, merging harmoniously into the park in which it is set. This easy harmony between the palace and the park is largely due to the splendid double colonnade in the Corinthian order which links the projecting elements of the building. The colonnade itself is a masterpiece of architectural skill.

Quarenghi also designed many buildings in the suburbs of St Petersburg, as well as in Moscow and other towns. The classical sobriety and formality of his work was very much in the spirit of the time, and the buildings he designed stood out even in a period of great architectural achievement as a permanent contribution to the architectural heritage of Russia.

Another foreigner who occupies a prominent place in the history of Russian architecture is the Scottish architect Charles Cameron (1740s to 1812), who did much work in the immediate surroundings of St Petersburg, including in particular the Agate Pavilion, the Hanging Gardens and the galleries at Tsarskoe Selo (now Pushkin) and a palace at Pavlovsk. Cameron's style is seen at its best in the interiors of his palaces, where the intricate design of moulded ornament and parquet flooring offered scope for his exquisite taste and his delicate sense of style.

Among many other architects who did good work during this period were Vincenzo Brenna, Egor Sokolov and Ivan Egorov.

The last thirty years of the 18th century were thus a period of great achievement in the history of Russian architecture. They were also a time of remarkable progress in urban development, during which new principles of town planning were established and great advances were made in the art of landscape gardening.

Thus Russian art could look back on a long and fruitful course of development during the 18th century, a period of steady advance and great achievement. The century was notable for the establishment of a new materialistic ideology, the abandonment of the old mediaeval dogmas, and the creation of a secular and realistic school of art. This process had begun in an earlier century, but it acquired a particular impetus and direction in the Petrine period.

Religious art did not, however, disappear in the 18th century: it was neither destroyed nor prohibited. As in earlier times, icons were painted and churches were decorated; as in earlier times, the building of churches continued, and successive generations of craftsmen devoted their skill to handing on the traditions of these older arts. But in the new conditions religious art lost its former pre-eminence retreated before the advance of secular art, and underwent significant change. The whole of religious art came under the influence of the trend towards realism, and icon-painting increasingly lost its former monumentality and schematism.

The vigorous forward movement of Russian art and its full measure of achievement were demonstrated in many ways, not least in the high standards of professional skill attained by Russian artists and craftsmen. Rejecting the conventionality and schematism of mediaeval views on artistic creation, they gained a new vision of the world, a new conception of the rôle of art in human life, a new understanding of form.

Russian art reflected the enhanced significance now accorded to human personality, in fundamental contrast to the mediaeval attitude. Man now achieved a deeper understanding of the world around him, no longer seeking in it manifestations of the divine will but rather striving to use it for his own purposes and bring it under the control of human reason.

The realistic approach which now became the dominant strain in Russian art led to the emergence of new genres, which previously had either not existed or had not developed beyond a rudimentary stage. Portrait painting advanced to a leading position; its aim was now to reveal the inmost essence of human personality, to establish its individual validity and its independence of any association with class, to demonstrate its manysidedness and its profound significance.

Russian art, as exemplified particularly in architecture, sculpture and historical painting, was permeated with a consciousness of human rights and obligations, a mood of patriotic fervour, a sense of social duty — trends which were to be further developed in the following century. This concern with human rights and duties was a consequence of the increasing national and social awareness of Russian society, the further strengthening of government organisation, and the advance of the Enlightenment.

The foreign artists who came to Russia at the beginning of the 18th century occupied a place of some prominence in the artistic life of the country. They found a ready market for their talents and achieved a degree of prosperity which was denied to the Russian artists of the day. In the second half of the century, however, the situation underwent a radical change. The artists turned out by the new Academy of Arts rapidly demonstrated their superiority and obtained European recognition; and Russian artists now began to be entrusted with commissions of increasing importance and to give striking evidence of their high standards of professional accomplishment.

The distinctive characteristic of 18th century Russian art is the urgent pace of its advance. Never before had the various genres developed so rapidly; never before had new and progressive ideas obtained such ready acceptance over so wide a field.

Silver binding of an aurochs horn.
From the "Black Tomb" kurgan near Chernigov. 10th century.
Historical Museum, Moscow (Ph. Novosti).

List of Illustrations

Contents

Printed in July 1976
On the Presses of Nagel Publishers, Geneva

The binding was executed
In the Workshops of Nagel Publishers, Geneva

The Publisher's legal deposit number is 689

Printed in Switzerland